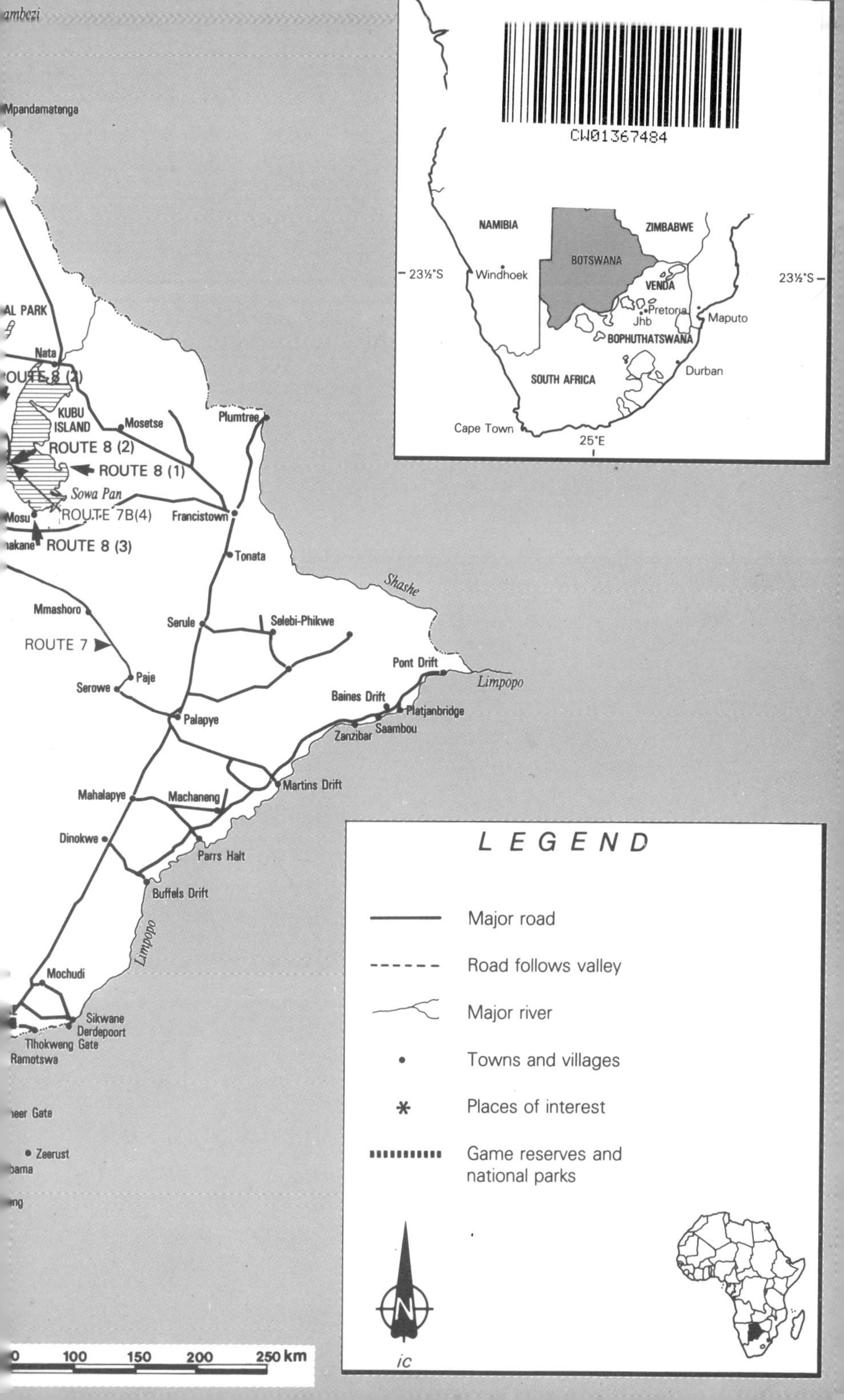
ambezi
Mpandamatenga
AL PARK
Nata
OUTE 8 (2)
KUBU ISLAND
Mosetse
Plumtree
ROUTE 8 (2)
ROUTE 8 (1)
Sowa Pan
ROUTE 7B(4)
Mosu
Francistown
akane
ROUTE 8 (3)
Tonata
Shashe
Mmashoro
Serule
Selebi-Phikwe
ROUTE 7
Paje
Serowe
Pont Drift
Limpopo
Baines Drift
Platjanbridge
Palapye
Saambou
Zanzibar
Martins Drift
Mahalapye
Machaneng
Dinokwe
Parrs Halt
Buffels Drift
Limpopo
Mochudi
Sikwane
Derdepoort
Tlhokweng Gate
Ramotswa
eer Gate
Zeerust
bama
eng
0
100
150
200
250 km
NAMIBIA
ZIMBABWE
BOTSWANA
23½°S
Windhoek
VENDA
Pretoria
Jhb
Maputo
BOPHUTHATSWANA
SOUTH AFRICA
Durban
Cape Town
25°E
LEGEND
Major road
Road follows valley
Major river
Towns and villages
Places of interest
Game reserves and national parks
N
ic

Bechuanaland

VISITORS' GUIDE TO BOTSWANA

VISITORS' GUIDE TO BOTSWANA

HOW TO GET THERE · WHAT TO SEE · WHERE TO STAY

Mike Main, Sandra and John Fowkes

SOUTHERN
BOOK PUBLISHERS

Visitors' Guide to Botswana
Copyright © 1987 by the authors

All rights reserved. No part of this publication may be reproduced or transmitted in any form or by any means without prior written permission from the publisher.

ISBN 1 86812 485 1

First edition, first impression 1987
First edition, second impression 1988
This edition published jointly by
Southern Book Publishers SA
Hunter Publishing USA
Moorland Publishing UK 1993

Southern Book Publishers (Pty) Ltd
P.O. Box 3103, Halfway House, 1685
South Africa

Published in the USA by
Hunter Publishing, Inc
300 Ratitan Centre Parkway
Edison NJ 08818
(908) 225 1900 Fax (908) 417 0842

Published in the UK by
Moorland Publishing Co Ltd
Moor Farm Road West
Airfield Estate
Ashbourne
Derbyshire
DE6 1HD

ISBN 0 86190 272 6

Cover design by Insight Graphics
Maps by Ingrid Cornelius
Set in 10 on 11½ pt Palatino
by Kohler Carton & Print, Natal
Printed and bound by Kohler Carton & Print, Natal

PREFACE

Who are we and why have we produced this guidebook to Botswana?

This book has been born out of the authors' many years of wandering in Botswana, delighting in the pristine and unspoilt environment, the people and the ambience of the country. In the decade spanning our visits we have seen significant changes, many of them a source of concern and which led us to become more deeply involved in Botswana in different ways. John and Sandra undertook a study of the contribution of tourism to the economy of Botswana, and Mike spent eighteen months researching and writing a book on the Kalahari. In the course of these studies we gathered a vast amount of information and became constant sources of reference for people wanting to travel to Botswana. The guidebook had in fact started writing itself but it took a while for us to realise that it already existed and merely needed to be written down.

All three authors have a strong interest in conservation. We are all aware of the irony that one of the greatest dangers to any unspoilt environment is the people who try to protect it. We realise, too, that the very fact that there is a guidebook to the wildlands of Botswana may mean that they will soon no longer be the isolated places they once were.

Of those who consult this book, those who seek the soul solace of earth untrammeled by city man, we ask only this: Be thoughtful of your actions that you might not so selfishly enjoy and use the wild areas that you destroy or change them for those who will follow you.

THE AUTHORS

ACKNOWLEDGEMENTS

We owe a debt of gratitude to many for this book.

To Ian and Jean Marshall, whose open house hospitality over so many years made Gaborone a good place to be in.

To Alec Campbell, friend, mentor, and guide and a constant fund of knowledge and insight.

To the Kalahari Conservation Society which, from its concern for wise land use planning in Botswana, supported the continuation of John's research on tourism and led to three incredible months of exploration.

To Lally Warren, a Motswana who showed us the 'Tswana way' and gave insights into the soul of the Batswana and their land.

To the many people whose generous hospitality and freely given assistance and time have made all our wanderings in Botswana such a delight.

Last, but not least, to the variety of vehicles which have carried us so many miles through Botswana without serious mishap. That this happened is, in no small measure, due to the craftsmanship of Phillip Welch and his ability to diagnose and fix the mysterious problems that beset the innards of motor vehicles.

Because of these people we travelled again and again to the magic places of Botswana. Without them, therefore, this guide could never have been written.

To those who would wish to improve the accuracy of future editions of this book: we would welcome your comments, updates, etc. Please send them to us, care of the publishers:

Southern Book Publishers (Pty) Ltd
PO Box 3103
Halfway House
1685

CONTENTS

Introduction 1
How to use this guide 2

1. PLACES TO VISIT 3
Aha Hills 3
Bokspits 4
Chobe National Park (river front) 5
Deception Valley 5
Drotsky's Cave 6
Ghanzi (town and district) 7
Kalahari Gemsbok National Park 8
Khutse Game Reserve 9
Lake Ngami 10
Mabuasehube Game Reserve 11
Makgadikgadi Game Reserve 12
Moremi Wildlife Reserve 13
Ntwetwe Pan 14
Nxai Pan National Park 16
Okavango Delta 17
Savuti and Mababe 18
Sowa Pan 20
Tshane/Hukuntsi Cluster of Villages 23
Tsodilo Hills 23
Western Woodlands (Masetlheng Pan) 25

2. HOW TO GET THERE 26
Some common routes for two- and four-wheel-drive vehicles . 27
   Two-wheel-drive vehicles 27
   Four-wheel-drive vehicles (a two-week trip) 28
   Four-wheel-drive vehicles (a three-week trip) 28
Detailed routes 30
   Route 1: Gaborone–Khutse Game Reserve 30
   Route 2: Gaborone–Mabuasehube Game Reserve 30
   Route 3: Gaborone–Ghanzi 31
   Route 4: Jwaneng–Sekoma–Khakhea–Werda 33

Route 5: Werda–Bokspits 34
Route 6: Kang–Tshabong 35
Route 6A: Hukuntsi–Western Woodlands (Masetlheng Pan) . 35
Route 7: Serowe–Orapa 36
Route 7A: Mopipi–Deception Valley 37
Route 7B: Ntwetwe Pan 38
   Part 1 – Orapa to Gweta 38
   Part 2 – The Western Islands 40
   Part 3 – Nata-Maun Road to Gabasadi Island 40
   Part 4 – Kubu Island to Gweta 41
Route 8: Sowa Pan 41
   Part 1 – East of Sowa Pan 41
   Part 2 – West of Sowa Pan 42
   Part 3 – South of Sowa Pan 45
Route 9: Francistown–Maun 45
Route 10: Makgadikgadi Game Reserve from Nata-Maun road 46
Route 11: Nxai Pan from Nata-Maun road and Baines' Baobabs 48
Route 12: Maun–Ghanzi 49
Route 13: Ghanzi–Mamuno 50
Route 14: Maun–Lake Ngami 50
Route 15: Maun–Drotsky's Cave 51
Route 16: Drotsky's Cave–Aha Hills 52
Route 17: Maun–Tsodilo 52
Route 18: Maun–Moremi–Savuti 53
Route 19: Savuti–Kasane 55
Botswana distance chart 56

3. FACTORS AFFECTING YOUR CHOICE 57
Seasons and climate 57
Best times to visit the parks and reserves 58
Children in the bush 60
Birdlife: where and when 61
Fishing: where and when 62

4. PREPARING FOR THE TRIP 64
What to take 64
   Accessories 64
   Clothing 65
   Shoes 66
Health precautions 66

Diseases	66
Venoms	69
Other	70
First aid	70
Vehicle spares	71
Maps	71
Packing your vehicle	72
Food and drink	73
Camping gear	74
Cooking utensils and other basic equipment	75
Clothing	76

5. CUSTOMS ... 77

Border posts	77
Airports	78
Customs requirements for visitors	78
Firearms	79
Boats	79
Road tax	79
Currency	79
Health certificates	80
Visa requirements	80
Pets	80
Length of stay	81
Motor vehicles: licences and insurance	81

6. DRIVING AND YOUR VEHICLE ... 82

Speed limits	82
Safety belts	82
Hazards	82
Accidents	83
Vehicle breakdowns	84
Jacking up a vehicle	84
Stuck on a clay pan	84
Flat battery	85
Clutch and brake fluid	85
Slave or master cylinder goes	85
Bush behaviour	85
When driving	86
When camping	86

Bush driving 88
    Gears 89
    Steering 90
    Tyre pressure 90
    Radiators and grass seeds 90
    Driving through water 91
    Gravel roads 91
    Driving after dark 92

7. FACILITIES 93
Facilities in national parks and reserves 93
Park entry fees and regulations 95
Where to stay in Botswana 97
Hotels 97
Lodges 101
    List of lodges 101
    Francistown area 102
    Gweta area 103
    Kasane area 105
    Maun area 109
    Moremi area 114
    Savuti area 126
    Nata area 131
    Tuli area 132
    Western Delta area 137
Campsites in national parks 142
    Chobe National Park 143
    Moremi Wildlife Reserve 144
    Nxai Pan National Park 145
    Makgadikgadi Game Reserve 145
Mobile safari operators 146
    Starting points 146
    List of known Mobile Safari Operators 147
    Factors affecting price 149

8. MISCELLANEOUS INFORMATION 151
Aircraft charter and maintenance 151
Banks in Botswana 152
Diplomatic representatives resident in Botswana 152
    Consular offices and trade missions based in Botswana . . . 153

International organisations based in Botswana	154
Entertainment	154
Government offices and hours	154
Language and customs	155
Petrol and diesel	156
Professional services	157
Public holidays	158
Public transport	159
Air	159
Buses	159
Rail	160
Hitch-hiking	160
Reference material	160
Service organisations and societies	162
Shopping	163
Telephone system	164
Travel agencies	165
Vehicle hire	166
MAPS OF TOWNS	168
Ghanzi	168
Gaborone	169
Maun	170
Kasane/Kazungula	171
Francistown	172
Selebi–Phikwe	173
Lobatse	174
INDEX	175

INTRODUCTION

Botswana is a very special place, rightly renowned for its wildlife. It is the big animals which immediately come to mind and on a visit to the national parks of Moremi and Chobe, for example, you are likely to see many different kinds of antelope, elephant and hippo, giraffe, lion, jackal and hyena, monkeys and baboons. With luck you could see leopard, cheetah and rhinoceros. If you delight in birds you won't be disappointed, and you will keep your companions entertained as they witness your dilemma in choosing between picking up binoculars to get a better look at a new bird, a camera to photograph another and a bird book to try to find out what both are!

If your wildlife interests are even more specialised, Botswana offers a great diversity of plants, insects and reptiles. Some are as yet unnamed – and could even bear your name if you introduce them to science.

Add to this array of plants and animals a unique geographical feature, the Okavango Delta, where a river runs into a semi-desert, spills its contents over a surface area of 13 000 km^2 of waterways and then quietly disappears under the thirsty sands, and you have another reason to explore Botswana. Throw in the Kalahari Desert and the Makgadikgadi Pans and the reasons multiply.

Although the Okavango Delta is perhaps the most popular area, Botswana has a great deal more to offer. The Kalahari Desert that finally swallows the waters of the Okavango River holds strong attraction and the diverse people of the country are another good reason to visit it.

Contrast and new experiences must be two of the main reasons for travel. You will not find many countries on the African continent that contrast so strongly with the urban environment of the average American or European traveller than does Botswana.

HOW TO USE THIS GUIDE

This book grew out of the authors' experience in answering people's questions on how to get to Botswana and what to do when they got there.

It is written primarily for the person who is travelling in a private party, not with a tour operator, although there is a section in Chapter 7 on the operators who take tours through Botswana.

Before planning your trip, turn to Chapter 1. This covers the places to visit and the routes that can be used to get there. Then work out the time you have available, decide on the way you want to travel (ie with your own two-wheel-drive or four-wheel-drive vehicle or with an operator) and the things that interest you most.

This information will give your trip a shape. Now you can look at where on your route to stay.

Finally, there are plenty of useful tips on what to carry with you, what you can expect at the border posts and ways of communicating with the Batswana.

Maps appear on pages 100 and 134, and town plans on pages 168-173.

1. PLACES TO VISIT

Botswana offers the visitor some remarkable and interesting places. Some are of scenic beauty, some are of cultural or historical interest. Many are well known, others less so. Whatever your reason for visiting the country, whether it be the game or the birdlife, to obtain an understanding of what conditions are really like in the Kalahari, or to experience for yourself the freedom of total isolation, you can be sure that your visit will be memorable and worthwhile. This list does not pretend to describe every place of interest. Botswana is sufficiently little known for you to be able to make your own discoveries – a factor which adds to its many attractions.

AHA HILLS (Routes 15 and 16)

Of all the places of interest in Botswana, the Aha Hills are probably the most remote and difficult of access. However, their isolation and their incongruous existence in the very centre of a vast dune-field lend a certain fascination. Straddling the border with Namibia, the Aha Hills consist almost entirely of limestone, dolomite and marble and form a low plateau some 245 km^2 in extent. The rocks are approximately 700 million years old. It is said that the name for the hills comes from the onomatopoeic Bushman word for the barking gecko which is so abundant in the area.

In addition to magnificent views of real Kalahari country, the hills offer the excitement of a largely unexplored area. Although only 50 km from Drotsky's Cave in the Kwihabe Hills, and of the same material, it is not known to what extent similar cave formations exist at Aha. Such exploration as has taken place has shown the existence of two sink-holes, about 15 km apart but apparently unrelated to each other. Both holes are vertical and dangerous. One is believed to be about 55 m deep although the bottom has not yet been reached. The other is about 35 m deep. Persons without experience or proper equipment are strongly advised against investigating them.

About 15 km south of Aha is the village of Xai Xai, and approximately 60 km to the north are the village and area of Dobe. At both places settlements of Tawana people and Bushmen can be found. It was at

Dobe that much work was undertaken by American research teams on the Bushmen residents, their findings later being published in many authoritative works. To some extent, that work continues and interesting archaeological research is being carried out in the area today. Both Middle and Late Stone Age sites have been located and, as at Drotsky's Cave, abundant evidence is being found of previous climatic regimes.

Only the most limited range of commodities is available at the stores in Xai Xai and other villages along the way. There is no standing water at Aha although the wells of the villagers may usually be relied upon. The nearest petrol, after Maun, is at Etsha (out of drums from the main village, Etsha 6), Shakawe (from Barrie Pryce at Shakawe Fishing Camp) and at Andara in the Caprivi Strip. Visitors must be entirely self-sufficient. Some traffic does use the main roads but vehicles are very infrequent, so it is advisable to be prepared for any eventuality.

Further information regarding the location of Aha's sink-holes can be obtained from the offices of the Botswana Society, National Museum, Gaborone in whose publication, *Botswana Notes and Records*, Vol 6, 1974, more details can be found.

BOKSPITS (Routes 3, 4 and 5)

The unusual name of this small village, set in the most south-westerly corner of Botswana, comes simply from being the place where a man called Bok once sank a well. Today it is a centre of karakul production. Petrol and diesel are available here and there is a police station, clinic and a well-stocked store.

Few would disagree that 'Mr Bokspits', the unofficial mayor, is Klaas van der Westhuizen and if anybody needs help or assistance, Klaas is the man to see. He will willingly introduce you to local farmers if you would like to know more about the karakul industry in the area. In addition, he'll demonstrate his remarkable powers of water-divining!

There are large, red, mobile sand dunes in the vicinity of Bokspits, which make fascinating subjects for photographers. Approximately 20 km to the east is Rappel's Pan which provides an excellent opportunity to investigate these curious features of the Kalahari (see Mabuasehube). Provided one stays on the main roads there is no need for a four-wheel-drive vehicle.

CHOBE NATIONAL PARK (RIVER FRONT)

Served by the tarred road from Francistown, the Kasane/Chobe area is becoming increasingly popular with the motorist. This has both disadvantages and attractions. Whilst on the one hand it is easier to get there – and the whole journey, including a visit to the northern part of the park, can be completed in a standard vehicle – the park's facilities are often overcrowded, especially during school holidays.

Perhaps the greatest attraction of the Chobe River area is the elephants which are almost always seen there. Their late afternoon visits to the water's edge offer hours of fascinating viewing and wonderful opportunities for the photographer. It is well, however, to be extremely cautious with Chobe's elephants. Often the herds consist mainly of females with young. The cows are sensitive to interference and more than one incident has been recorded where a vehicle has been damaged after an imprudent approach.

The drier months are the best time to visit Chobe, when the animals are driven back to the river through want of water in the hinterland. Huge numbers will be seen, particularly of elephant and buffalo. You can also expect to see tsessebe, waterbuck, roan, eland, sable, giraffe, rhinoceros and, if you are lucky, one of the rare puku. The floodplains of the river make an ideal viewing area, with mixed patches of open grassland, thickets of bush and riverine forest. In the river itself you should see hippo, crocodile and, with patient watching, the wonderful otters.

DECEPTION VALLEY (Route 7A from Routes 7 and 10)

Mark and Delia Owens brought this area to the notice of the public with their popular book *Cry of the Kalahari* and many people have wanted to visit it.

It lies on the north-eastern edge of the Central Kalahari Game Reserve, an area now open to the general public and subject to Botswana's park fees although it is totally undeveloped.

Evocative word pictures of this wilderness are too widely known to need repeating here. Suffice it to say that Deception Valley itself and the pans in its vicinity will often have game on them. Even without animals, the area reflects so faithfully the peace and immeasurable qualities that tipify the true Kalahari that any visitor will find himself amply rewarded for the journey.

Be warned, though; to venture here alone is considered by many to be foolish. Few vehicles use the track that will get you there. Game scouts are not always present. A breakdown or other emergency will leave you isolated and a long way from help.

DROTSKY'S CAVE (Route 15)

In western Botswana, not far from the Namibian border, is a remarkable series of caves, shown by the Bushmen to Martinus Drotsky in 1934.

Perhaps not as extensive as the better known Cango Caves in South Africa, Drotsky's can certainly equal any with the truly breathtaking splendour of its stalagmites, stalactites, flowstones, caverns and passages. It has, for some, an additional attraction in that it is quite unspoilt and undeveloped. Apart from their scenic attraction, the caves are of great interest to geomorphologists and palaeo-climatologists because of the abundant evidence they provide of former climates.

As is so often the case in Botswana, the approach and surroundings leave one quite unprepared for the splendour that is to come. Set in an apparently endless dune-field of rolling, arid country, a low outcrop of dolomite barely protrudes above the ubiquitous sand on the banks of the now dry Kwihabe River. Yet once this river flowed, and flowed strongly. There was sufficient water about physically to dissolve the rock itself, to carve out the great winding passages and caverns. At other, slightly drier times, falling rain percolated through the dolomite, forming and shaping striking displays of white flowstone or cave sinter.

The age of the caves is not known and the date of the earliest phases of solution, speculative. There is, however, more certain evidence for a very wet period between 17 000 and 14 000 years ago, sufficiently wet in fact to flood and re-excavate the old passages. Drier times returned and some of the flowstones were deposited, to be partly eroded during a subsequent wet period about 4 500 years ago. A succession of wet and dry periods followed, including at least one especially wet period when the most recent of the cave sinters were deposited, between 2 000 and 1 500 years ago.

There are two entrances to the cave. The track will lead you to one which is 300 m from the right-hand bank of the river, on the slopes of the low hill. Beside it is a large information board, erected by the National Museum. The second entrance is 200 m away from the first in a direction at right angles to the river valley and further from it.

There are no facilities at Drotsky's. There are no people living in the immediate vicinity. There is no water at all, not even in the caves themselves. Take care, therefore, to be entirely self-sufficient. The nearest reliable fuel is Maun but you may find petrol at Gumare (where a licence has been applied for) or at Etsha 6 (where it is sold from drums). A minimum of two full days is recommended to explore the area properly. Game, because of the lack of water, is seasonally rare and the chance of encountering any large predators is remote.

The caves can be dangerous. There is, of course, no lighting, natural or artificial, so you must take your own. Gas lamps are useful and torches are essential. You will make constant use of your lights so ensure that you have plenty of spare gas and batteries.

Never enter the caves without a secondary, emergency light supply on your person, eg matches or a small torch. This precaution is absolutely essential. Should a light be put down and go out, a very serious situation could develop.

Previous explorers of the cave have left strings marking the main routes. Some sections have been removed but the remainder serve as a guide. It is possible to go in one entrance and out the other but a good knowledge of the system is required in order to do this.

Photographers are advised to equip themselves with more than one flash, preferably slave units mounted on tripods. Three standard flashes will provide sufficient light. Dust within the caves is a major problem. It hangs in the air for long periods of time and special care should be taken to protect sensitive equipment.

Plans of the cave are available from the Botswana Society, National Museum, Gaborone, in whose journal *Botswana Notes and Records*, Vol 6, 1974, they will be found.

GHANZI (Routes 2 and 3)

The frontier town of Ghanzi in the west of Botswana consists of a small and thriving community. Today it is the centre of a substantial cattle ranching industry. Deep in the Kalahari, it owes its unlikely success to the limestone ridge on which it is situated, providing as it does an abundant supply of groundwater for most of the 190 farms that now exist there.

Originally the home of Bushmen, Ghanzi has seen many people come and go. The first white inhabitant was the extraordinary Hendrik van

Zyl, who took up permanent residence in 1874 on what is today Ghanzi Farm Number One. Tales of his exploits and lifestyle abound – his double-storeyed house with its French furniture and stained glass windows, his murder of thirty-three Bushmen, and the slaughter of 103 elephants in a single afternoon. A feature known as Van Zyl's Cutting is attributed to him but its purpose is uncertain. Cut 3 m deep into solid rock and nearly 12 m long, some people today believe it was a reservoir to catch rainwater. By this means, it is thought, Van Zyl was able to extend his hunting in the area, sure of a dependable water supply. It is difficult now to separate fact from fancy but Van Zyl certainly seems to have been a law unto himself.

The ill-fated Dorsland Trekkers reached Ghanzi in late 1875 but soon moved on to their sad future in Namibia and Angola.

Next to arrive were the Rhodes' Trekkers, the first of whom reached the area in October 1898. Ten years later all but one family had left. The descendants of that family and others who drifted into the struggling settlement in those early years, remain in Ghanzi today where they form the strong Afrikaans- and English-speaking communities.

Today Ghanzi is prosperous. Land prices have improved, as has the quality of the herd and management practices. The town is a busy administrative centre but, more important, it is a pleasing testimony to the ability of widely disparate and strongly independent peoples to live together equably and in harmony.

The ruins of Van Zyl's house can still be found on Dick Eaton's farm, Ghanzi One. Van Zyl's Cutting is on Dagga Camp farm, about 60 km from Ghanzi, owned by the Vosloos. Owners must be contacted for permission to enter the farms. The management at the Kalahari Arms Hotel in Ghanzi will assist in organising this. Ghanzi can provide all basic necessities and has a hospital, as well as radio/telephone contact with the rest of the country.

KALAHARI GEMSBOK NATIONAL PARK (Routes 3, 4 and 5)

The standard point of entry to this park is through South Africa, via Bokspits and Twee Rivieren. There is, however, a road north from Bokspits with a gate into the park on the Botswana side of the border and Botswana's Department of Wildlife and National Parks now have a warden and staff stationed within the Kalahari Gemsbok.

Access from the Botswana side is, therefore, possible. However, use of this facility is not encouraged at the moment since there is no infrastructure for visitors. Persons explicitly wishing to enter the park through Botswana should write for permission to do so to the Director, Dept of Wildlife and National Parks, PO Box 131, Gaborone, Tel (267) 371405. Otherwise all normal entry will continue, for the time being, to be from South Africa through Twee Rivieren.

It should also be noted that, although some maps continue to indicate it, there is no exit from the park at Union's End. The gate there has been closed for many years.

A visit to the Kalahari Gemsbok does not require a four-wheel-drive vehicle. The park is open all the year round.

From Bokspits one needs to enter South Africa at the border post, which is open from 8 am to 4 pm, and take the excellent dirt road north for 55 km to the park entrance at Twee Rivieren Camp. Entrance formalities are completed here. There is a shop selling essentials and fuel, and there are camping and residential facilities at the camp.

There are three main sand roads in the park. All are maintained in first rate condition. One extends for 157 km up the Nossob River to Nossob Camp and then 128 km beyond it, on the same river, to the closed gate at Union's End. A second road runs beside the Aoub River for 118 km to the Namibian entrance gate and camp at Mata Mata. A link road of 68 km joins the two river roads and affords excellent views of the drier Kalahari with its typical stabilised, red dunes. Fuel and basic essentials are also sold at both Mata Mata and Nossob camps.

The park has a fluctuating population of game but a visit is always well rewarded. At least two days is recommended, during which you can expect to see gemsbok, wildebeest, eland, hartebeest and springbok, as well as lion, cheetah, hyena and jackal.

KHUTSE GAME RESERVE (Route 1)

This relatively small game reserve (2 500 km^2) is the closest of Botswana's reserves and parks to Gaborone. Set in typical pan country of undulating savannah, it abuts the vast Central Kalahari Game Reserve to the north.

Most of the larger arid-adapted herbivores can be found in Khutse Reserve, together with the more common predators, including lion, leopard and cheetah. Game is usually seen on or near the pans (of which there are more than sixty, large and small), but it is seasonal. Its presence will depend much on where and when the rain last fell and it is difficult to predict. If there has been a drought, game may be very scarce, if not completely absent. In the absence of larger animals there is an abundance of smaller creatures and Khutse is renowned for its birdlife. There is, of course, the special atmosphere of the countryside itself. The Kalahari is unique and a visit to Khutse allows the visitor to savour its silence and fascinating immensity.

Entrance to the reserve requires a fee for vehicle and passengers. Campsites have been laid out and, although water is available at the gate, it is fairly salty and visitors are advised to bring their own. A guide can be taken on but it is not really necessary to do so. There is only a single road into the reserve. It forks at Khutse II Pan, 13 km from the gate. The left-hand road extends 53 km to Moreswe Pan; the right-hand side remains for 16 km in the reserve and then continues to a distant mining concession. No maps are currently available at the gate but it is wise to make a hand-drawn copy of the one on display.

LAKE NGAMI (Route 14)

A four-wheel-drive vehicle is not essential for a visit to Lake Ngami but it is strongly recommended. There are no facilities beyond the limited range of goods available in the occasional small general dealer's store.

Lake Ngami has spawned a host of myths and it remains to this day something of an enigma. It is a lake with no exit and survives on overflow from the Okavango Delta. There is good evidence that levels once were much higher, and enclosed a huge area of 1 800 km^2. By the time Livingstone saw the lake on 1 August 1849, it had already lost its former glory and it is unlikely to have been more than 810 km^2 in extent. He described it as 'a fine looking sheet of water' and estimated the circumference at 120 km. Progressively, as the years passed, the supply of water diminished and the levels fluctuated around a much lower mean. Often it was quite dry for long periods. In the last hundred years Ngami has been but a faint shadow of its former self, barely exceeding 250 km^2 in area.

The dynamics of Ngami's inflows are now better understood and it seems clear that the gradual drying up of the Thaoge River is the main reason for its diminution in size since Livingstone's day. The reasons for the Thaoge's demise are more controversial. However, the weight of opinion now seems to favour a change in the levels of the tectonically unstable Okavango Delta. Like a giant tabletop, it may have tipped slowly in a different direction, altering the flow pattern of the waters spread across its surface.

Lake Ngami remains the centre of an important cattle raising area for the Tawana and Herero people. Estimates of the total number of cattle supported by the lake flats and surrounding areas vary from 30 000 to 70 000 head, but some consider this far too high a figure, and it is true that there are dramatic collapses in the cattle population when drought occurs.

MABUASEHUBE GAME RESERVE (Route 2)

Across the southern third of Botswana, from east to west, runs a ridge of land marginally higher than that to the north or south. S Parssarge, a German geologist and explorer, called it the Bakalahari Schwelle and, indeed, it is a gigantic watershed. Characteristically, it is dotted with many thousands of pans.

These features vary in shape but most are oval or circular. Typically there is a high sand dune, or series of dunes, on the south or southwest side. Some are as much as 20 or 30 m high. The pans, some of which hold water for a few months of the year, range from bare, salty clay to being lightly covered with grasses. They play a vital role in the ecology of the area and have also played an important part in man's invasion of the Kalahari, providing him with access to water and grazing for his animals. It was partly recognition of these facts that led to the establishment of Mabuasehube Game Reserve in the south of the country.

Remote and costly in terms of time and fuel, the reserve is nevertheless well worth a visit. The simple beauty of the stark pans, the extraordinary colour changes that occur as the day progresses, and the often abundant game will make it a unique and memorable visit.

Mabuasehube is not fenced but an entrance fee is required. The ranger in residence has access to borehole water but this should not be relied upon. There are six major pans within the reserve as well as many smaller ones. During the rainy season, from October to April, wildebeest, gemsbok, springbok, hartebeest and eland, with their associated predators, usually abound. Only towards the really dry times do they migrate in search of surface water.

There are no facilities of any kind in the reserve and the visitor must be entirely self-sufficient. The nearest fuel is at Tsabong, a District Headquarters, 110 km away. On the approach, the last fuel stops are at Jwaneng or at Werda. Both centres have shopping facilities and there is a store at Khakhea.

It is recommended that at least two full days should be allowed in the reserve to appreciate all that it has to offer.

MAKGADIKGADI GAME RESERVE (Route 10)

This reserve is a vast unfenced area (3 900 km^2) of open plain and bush country to the south of the main Francistown–Maun road, about halfway between the two centres. It is informally serviced by a series of unsignposted tracks, mapped on the notice board at the north entrance. A four-wheel-drive vehicle is not necessary but is advisable.

From June onwards, to about November or December, when the first rains have fallen, innumerable game will be encountered – herds of zebra and sometimes wildebeest – that seem to stretch from horizon to horizon. Each draws in its wake lion and other predators.

It is not only the game which is the attraction here, however, but the simple beauty of the area itself. The rolling grasslands seem endless. Early morning mirages build clear and distant mountain ranges which dissipate as the sun edges higher. Over the centuries shallow depressions in the plain accumulate deep deposits of clay and detritus. Into these reservoirs of richer soil, trees take root so that the plain is dotted with widely separated islands of vegetation. These islands create microhabitats as unique and varied as their ocean counterparts. If you are prepared to sit quietly for an hour or so on one of these islands, you will soon be accepted by the fauna and can enjoy the rare privilege of watching them go about their daily business.

Two localities in the game reserve are particularly worth visiting as they both make memorable camp sites. One is Njuca Hills, the other is Xhumaga on the Boteti River.

Njuca is an ancient dune of especially large proportions. A track leads up onto two locations where good camp sites with magnificent views are to be found, each equipped with its own 'whistle and thud' toilet.

To spend an evening or two here is to sample the real magic of the Kalahari as one watches the endless grasslands turn to gold and listens to the call of barking geckos as the sun takes its leave of another day, while, on the west of the site, a resident mongoose noses through your belongings for cheese, which it has come to adore.

On the east or left bank of the Boteti River, opposite a village called Xhumaga, the game scouts have a second camp and near it, under a group of shady acacias in a large sandy area overlooking the river, a new public campsite has been built. Here you will find one cold shower and one flush toilet. There is an adjacent stand-pipe which delivers fresh water and also a convenient pit for dumping rubbish.

The site itself is remarkable for its position in the ecotone between riverine woodland and the grasslands of Makgadikgadi. The birdlife is prolific and the scenery unusual for the Boteti is a river flowing to nowhere. Its waters simply soak away into the sand.

The visitor must be entirely self-sufficient in food and fuel. In addition he must collect and carry his own firewood which is singularly scarce at Njuca (the remaining trees are suffering accordingly) although supplies may be available at the Xhumaga campsite. We prefer to be independent and bring wood from further afield, thus reducing our impact on the immediate area.

MOREMI WILDLIFE RESERVE (Route 18)

This wildlife reserve was declared by the Tawana people in 1963, an act which was described at the time as a shining mark in African tribal history. Administered today by the Department of Wildlife and National Parks, it is a rich and fascinating area.

Located on the north-eastern side of the Okavango Delta, it encompasses several different types of ecological zones, adding greatly to its interest.

Entry is controlled by two gates, one in the north and another in the south. An entrance fee is required. A system of roads provides what is essentially a circular drive which allows the visitor to experience the ecological diversity of the reserve. It passes through dense mopani woodland, forests of giant acacia trees and in places skirts the edge of the Okavango with magnificent views of floodplains, reed banks and open lagoons. Animal and birdlife are prolific throughout the year but the drier months, from May to November, are best for viewing. At both entrances and at several locations along the road are designated campsites and it is well worth spending at least a night in this reserve. Mekoro (singular: mokoro) are not available for hire in Moremi.

You can expect to see most game animals in Moremi, including lion, leopard, elephant, eland, kudu and roan antelope, as well as buffalo, zebra and impala.

NTWETWE PAN (Route 7B)

This enormous and fascinating area, the twin in many ways of its easterly neighbour, Sowa Pan, has been receiving more and more attention from independent visitors. This is as it should be, for it is a gloriously free and open part of the country – ethereally beautiful and still almost completely unspoilt.

There are innumerable tracks and means of access to this area and it would be impractical to try and list them all – apart from the fact that this spoils the fun for intrepid explorers! In the section on routes, you will find a description of one major north–south track and another than enters the area from the south-east and establishes a link with Sowa Pan and the island of Kubu.

The region is full of places of great interest and we would like to highlight a few of them to encourage the exploration of this fascinating region.

A main track bisects the area from south to north, linking Orapa mine with Gweta. It is highly probable that it was along this very track that David Livingstone travelled on his journeys to Linyanti and the Caprivi Strip.

By means of this track it is possible to visit two famous baobab trees. The first, known as Green's Baobab, lies immediately beside the route. The tree is scarred with initials from a century or more ago, one of the earliest being that of trader and explorer Frederick Joseph Green.

Green had been hunting along the Boteti River as early as 1851 but in 1858/9, when his initials were carved into the bark of the tree, he, with his brother and a large group of wagons, was exploring the vicinity of Makgadikgadi whilst on their way to western Matabeleland.

The initials of H Van Zyl, the notorious explorer, hunter and murderer from what is now the Ghanzi District, are also to be found on this tree by the sharp-eyed and persistent.

Another equally famous, though less visited tree, Chapman's Baobab, lies south-east of Green's Tree. This colossal specimen, visible from great distances across the pan, is worth seeing if only because of its size and photogenic qualities. It is said that it was a landmark for the early explorers of the region, including one, if not more, of the Chapmans. It has yet to be systematically scrutinised for interesting signatures.

To the west of the north–south road is what we call the land of a thousand islands. Reflecting a chaotic climatic past, these numerous islands are in fact sand dunes stranded on the surface of the ancient lake-bed and they make one of the most wierdly fascinating places in Botswana.

The dunes are evidence of much more arid times when the lake temporarily dried and barchan dunes began to advance across its baked and bare surface. Eventually a wetter era returned, the lake flooded again and the dunes were trapped, islands in an ancient sea. But climatic change did not stop and the lake level fell once more, but incrementally this time, almost as if the water was struggling against the elemental forces that wished to banish it forever.

Proof of this struggle will be seen if you look carefully at the island profiles. Many of them show distinct steps and lines of vegetation, revealing clearly where the fall in lake levels was momentarily arrested for long enough to leave permanent evidence in the shape of ancient shorelines.

To drive through this area is a unique experience. The pan surface is hard and unyielding and, in our experience, very much safer than elsewhere on Makgadikgadi.

A good map is essential (see Routes) but, with its help and sitting on the roof of the vehicle for a good view, the experience is very much like sailing a galleon of old through unknown seas with islands beckoning from all about. It is both exhilirating and wildly exciting.

Careful navigation will lead you to a waterhole known as Mgobe wa Takhu in the north-west of the area which contains water for much of the year. To the north of the waterhole a little-known track will, in turn, deliver you to a group of palm trees known as Makolwane a ga Wateka, 10,6 km east of Njuca Hills (described under Route 10, p 46).

To the west of the south–north track that crosses Ntwetwe Pan and approximately midway between opposite shores, is the island of Gabasadi. An unusually large barchan dune, it is bare of vegetation but it is worth climbing to the (low) crest for the wonderful view of Ntwetwe that can be had.

It was here that Prince Charles, on a visit to Botswana, sat and painted his last picture before returning to England. He commented that it was so hot that his watercolours kept drying before he could spread them onto the paper!

Along the west shore of Ntwetwe that reaches down from the Nata–Maun road there are, as elsewhere on this pan, numerous Stone Age sites and among them, in a hidden cleft along the shore, is a secret waterhole that seldom dries. There are cattle at this particular place but game is also found there sometimes.

Around the hole are hunting blinds built of calcrete blocks and used by San of old who hid there to ambush game as it came down to drink. Along the access to this waterhole are stands of glorious aloes that bloom in winter and add a splash of unforgettable colour to the landscape.

This whole region is one that can absorb days of time for those with a penchant for 'beach walking', for exploring and for quietly encountering the 'non-game' wilderness at its unexploited best.

NXAI PAN NATIONAL PARK (Route 11)

A four-wheel-drive vehicle is necessary to get to this national park, which lies north of the Francistown–Maun road and is 36 km from it.

Nxai Pan National Park, recently enlarged to include Banies' Baobabs and the Kudiakam Pans, is set on the northern fringe of the Makgadikgadi basin and includes Nxai Pan, an ancient lake bed. There is a manned entrance gate and a fee for vehicle and passengers is required. There is no accommodation other than two campsites, one of which has an ablution block. Visitors are expected to be entirely self-sufficient, although water can usually be relied upon at the campsites. The game scouts will direct you to the campsites which are both within 10 km.

About 15 km to the east of the entrance, inside the park, is a large, unnamed pan complex. Kgama-Kgama Pan lies a further 9 km northeast of this complex. The pans themselves are the only parts to which there is ready access.

At certain times of the year, notably December to early April, if rains have fallen, game can be prolific and viewing spectacular. The area is a breeding ground for large herds of zebra, wildebeest, gemsbok, springbok and eland.

In the south of the national park is another complex of pans, the largest of which is Kudiakam. On a site overlooking this pan is a group of very large and impressive baobab trees, a picture of which was painted by Thomas Baines on 22 May 1862. Photographs taken in July 1967 scarcely show any discernible changes. Some people prefer camping among these trees to staying in the 'formal' campsite.

OKAVANGO DELTA

The Okavango Delta must truly be one of Africa's most enchanted places. A swirl of lushness in a desert of Kalahari sand, the Delta is a remarkable phenomenon. It owes its origins to the emergence of a rift valley across the course of the Okavango River. When exactly this occurred is not certain but, geologically speaking, it is likely to have been a relatively recent event. Certainly, the process is still developing and constant movement in the earth's crust may well explain the shifts in water distribution which are so much a feature of this remarkable area. In the aeons that have followed since the rift valley was formed, windblown sand and sediment delivered by the river have filled it and its floor now lies as much as 300 m below the fan-shaped delta that we see today.

A characteristic of the Delta is its annual flood. The Okavango, which rises in Angola, brings the result of heavy rains to Botswana's border. The swollen river breaches its low-water banks and begins again the annual inundation of its flood-plains. No two floods are ever the same but one can say that the permanent delta is some 6 000 km^2 in extent, whilst a big flood may seasonally cover as much as 13 000 km^2. In general, at Mohembo, where the Okavango enters Botswana, the flood begins as water levels rise from November onwards, but the peak is not reached until February or March, and it can take six months to work its way through the labyrinth of channels and lagoons to pass Maun. More than 95 per cent of the Okavango's water evaporates before it reaches the Thamalakane River which drains the area and leads the remainder to the Boteti and Lake rivers.

The flooding of the Okavango is not a violent process. The waters spread gently down the channels and across the plains. The total fall in height from one end of the Delta to the other is only 62 m, and that over a distance of some 250 km! The slow movement of water means a low sediment load and hence the incredible clarity and purity of the Okavango's water, for which it is justly renowned.

Unique as one of the world's few inland deltas, the Okavango adds enormously to the variety of experiences open to the visitor. Fishing is an obvious attraction, but game-viewing is also possible, if not on quite the same scale as in Chobe and Savuti. In addition one can take to the waters of this magic world of islands and lagoons by dugout canoe (mokoro) or power-boat. Aircraft can be hired and a flight across the Delta is a memorable experience.

It is difficult to enjoy the Okavango to the full without using the services of professional safari people. There are a number of reasons for this. Although the Delta is mapped, no practical map can hope to show the intricacies of the myriad channels. Indeed, many channels cannot be seen easily at all as they are overgrown with reeds. In order to find your way around successfully you will need a guide, someone who knows the area well. Also, you will want some kind of boat – and it would be a major undertaking to consider hauling your own boat to the Okavango for a short visit. All the services that you require can be arranged by any of the numerous safari camps and businesses found in Maun and elsewhere in the Delta, and it is best to make the necessary arrangements through them. These services include flights, hotels, camping, fishing, game-viewing, boat-hire and mokoro trips. A list of operators is given in Chapter 7.

SAVUTI AND MABABE (Route 18)

In the north of Botswana, well within the Chobe National Park, Savuti is perhaps one of the best known game-viewing areas in the country. Under ideal conditions the number and variety of animals seen can be quite staggering. Someone once described it as 'wall to wall game'!

Savuti is particularly known for its elephant and it seems to be an area preferred by lone bulls. More docile than the cow, these gentle giants are quite at home among the parked cars and campsites – they have been seen stepping delicately between the guy-ropes of tents! Be warned, though. Docility does not prevent these animals from seeking a little variety in their diet. One person had the boot of his car destroyed when a bull used his tusks as a tin-opener to get at the oranges he could smell inside. Under no circumstances feel tempted to feed the elephants.

Savuti's elephants are only one of its many attractions. Game viewing is at its best from November through to May, but if the Savuti Channel is flooded it can be good throughout the year. When the depression has received its first rain and has turned to a carpet of green, hundreds of thousands of animals are drawn to it. Zebra, impala, hartebeest, wildebeest, kudu, warthog, buffalo, rhinoceros, lion, leopard, hyena and jackal are but a few of the bewildering variety of animals to be seen. It is an experience of a lifetime.

The Mababe Depression, which stretches endlessly to the eastern horizon as a flat and featureless plain, is in fact the bed of a lake which once covered most of northern Botswana. As you drive into Savuti from the south you will see, on your left-hand side, a low sandy ridge. Called the Magwikhwe Sand Ridge, this feature, which is more than 100 km long, is an old barrier beach that may once have defined the western boundary of the great lake. Beyond it to the west is a chaotic pattern of ancient sand dunes which may have been an area of lagoons and mud flats.

It is still a matter for some speculation as to how this once massive lake received its waters. The most popular explanation is that once the Upper Zambezi, the Chobe and the Okavango rivers flowed together, across the north of Botswana and down to the sea via the Limpopo. A gentle warping of the earth's crust dammed this flow to create a vast lake. In time, however, further crustal movement caused these rivers to find a new route to the sea. Their direction changed by faulting, the Upper Zambezi and the Chobe turned to the north-east and, after plunging over the Victoria Falls, joined what is now the Middle Zambezi. Trapped by an emerging rift valley, the Okavango bled its waters into vast accumulations of sand, to create the delta we see today. Condemned by a changing climate which reduced rainfall and brought a return of almost desert-like conditions, the super-lake, cut off from its supplies of water, dried up and was no more.

Signs of the lake's existence are still abundant however. Apart from the obvious feature of the sand ridge, you will notice the nearly sheer north-eastern faces of the Gubatsaa Hills. These were cut into cliffs by the crashing force of the waves which once pounded against them. In the lee of the hills you will find accumulations of rounded gravel – pebbles that have been ground to their oval shape by ceaseless rolling on the shores of the lake.

One of the great mysteries and fascinations of Savuti is its famous channel. It runs a distance of 100 km from the Chobe River through a gap in the sand ridge, to the Mababe Depression. Falling only 20 cm for each kilometre of distance covered, this channel brings water from the Chobe to Mababe, creating a small marsh where it enters the Depression. It is the channel and its water which explain the fantastic abundance of game that can sometimes be seen at Savuti. However, the channel does not always flow and therein lies its great mystery.

We know from accounts of early explorers that it was flowing in the 1850s and until about 1880. At that time it ceased to flow and remained dry until the mid 1950s when, without explanation, it began to flow again. Since then, it has 'switched' on and off several times. At the moment it is dry. It is this quixotic flow that explains the dead trees you will see in the channel. They established themselves during the long dry period of this century and were killed off by the renewed flooding.

Even without water from the Chobe, Savuti remains a place of enchantment, of singular beauty, and boasts one of the greatest concentrations of animals in Southern Africa. It certainly is a place not to be missed on a visit to Botswana.

SOWA PAN (Route 8)

Sowa Pan can be explored, with care, experience and common sense, in an ordinary vehicle, but a four-wheel-drive vehicle is recommended. Heavy loads must be carried, as the whole area is quite isolated and offers no facilities whatsoever. You will need to provide your own water, food and fuel.

Sowa and its companion pan, Ntwetwe, to the west, together form the great Makgadikgadi Pans. These pans are all that is left today of a once great lake that covered most of northern Botswana.

The complete history of the lake is not yet known. It is unlikely to be older than two million years and may have held substantial quantities of water up to quite recent times. The most prolonged wet period for which there is good evidence was from 17 000 to 14 000 years ago. There were other such periods between 4 000 and 2 000 years before the present. To what extent these more moist conditions raised the lake levels, and what those levels were, still waits to be discovered. The most recent evidence suggests that the old lake bed might have been substantially flooded as recently as 1 500 years ago. It is certain, however, that levels have been as high as 40 m above the present lake bed.

Even today good rains will bring floods of water into the north-east and south-west of the Makgadikgadi Pans. When this happens water birds congregate in their millions and flamingos breed in the shallow waters.

There are places of indescribable beauty along the shores of these pans. Perhaps only a poet could really convey the feeling of tranquillity, space and freedom engendered by the immensity of these silvered pans and adjacent grasslands. Many such places remain to be discovered in this remote and enchanting wilderness, but those that are known are well worth visiting. One is Kubu Island.

This small rocky island, studded with grotesque yet appealing baobabs, has a unique ability to create a special atmosphere of its own. Its isolation, the starkness of its setting against the blinding infinity of the featureless pan, makes for a totally unique experience. Few who visit Kubu come away untouched by its magic. The island's appeal is not only to the senses. Near the survey beacon which marks its low summit, and set about it like a tonsure, lies a ring of rolled pebbles, which marks an old lake shore-line. At 919 m above sea level, it is one of the lower, and probably more recent levels, almost certainly within the last 20 000 years. The stone-wall ruins, the origins and secrets of which remain to be disclosed, add further mystery to the island.

To reach Kubu, find the turn-off described in Route 8, Part 2. From that point, the island is 19 km away. The track heads roughly north-east. Mostly you will be guided by previous vehicle tracks. Some claim that finding the island is easy and that often there is a 'highway' of tracks to follow. This may be true, but they do get washed away after the rains. In their absence, you will have to thread your way through the tussocked grass. Place a lookout on the roof, whose job it will be to watch for the low hillock that is Kubu. When sighted, do not drive directly towards it across the open pan unless you are following vehicle tracks. The surface can be very treacherous, especially during or after the rainy season, and it is difficult to extricate a vehicle that has sunk in deeply. Instead, like the churchmouse, work your way around the edge of open spaces, staying close to the grass. It will take a little longer to get there but you will at least arrive!

To the south of Kubu, and within sight if you look carefully, are two smaller islands. They suggest, even more eloquently than Kubu, the splendour and isolation of Sowa Pan. It is not wise to approach these islands directly, unless you are certain of the surface conditions. Again, the churchmouse technique is recommended. As it is, large expanses of bare pan must be crossed to reach them.

If at any stage while driving on the pan surface, you feel the vehicle sinking in, there are steps you can take that may help. First – pray! Second, do not do anything suddenly. Don't swing the steering wheel wildly, brake violently or accelerate harshly. A soft patch will create a distinct drag on the wheels. Collapse is heralded by the drag increasing to the point where the surface suddenly gives. Try and move away from the softer areas when drag is felt.

To the south-east of Sowa is the lesser known island of Kukonje or Kokoro. Directions to this island can be found in Route 8, Part 1. From the turn-off indicated you will see the island about 3 km from the shore. It is possible to drive across to it but you need confidence and experience to do so successfully, which only practice or a guide can give you. You are unlikely to find a local guide with the knowledge you need. The shortest approach is from the north, where the island is much closer to the mainland. You can drive around to this point, either by crossing the grassland or by 'churchmousing' round the edge. There is a shelf-beach in this area, and you can drive up it to a campsite which offers a magnificent view.

If you choose not to risk the drive, it does not take long to walk over to Kokoro. A beautiful island, it is gentler than Kubu. There are fossil beaches here, too, and at more than one locality are Late Stone Age sites.

If you should approach either of these islands from the south, and pass Mosu, it is worth turning into this village. There, set among tall palm trees, is a remarkable spring from which gushes clear, fresh water. Behind Mosu rises a towering escarpment, once the precipitous southern shore of the great lake. Now, alone in heat and silence, eddies of hot, dry wind swirl dust against its flanks where once cool waves washed.

In the north-east of Sowa Pan is the Nata River delta. Flowing from Zimbabwe, in a good wet season it may flood large areas to a shallow depth. Birdlife then is breathtaking. In the dry part of the year the grasslands invite you to explore. There is no game here; it is cattle country, as are all the grasslands around Sowa. Their presence detracts not at all, however, from the feeling of openness and freedom as you walk. And always, to the west, lies the limitless expanse of Sowa with its kaleidoscope of muted pastel colours, ever changing to reflect the passage of the sun through its day.

Sowa or Sua means salt and a major project to extract salt and soda ash is located on the eastern side of Sua Pan on the Sua spit. Forty wells pump salt brine from the underground aquifer system of the pan. The brine is pumped through an 82 km pipeline network to solar evaporation ponds covering an area of 25 km^2. The salt is recovered mechanically from the ponds but a further stage is needed to recover the soda ash via a chemical extraction process.

So major a project has clearly dramatically altered the character of part of the Sowa Pan.

TSHANE/HUKUNTSI CLUSTER OF VILLAGES (Routes 3 and 6)

Almost in the very centre of Botswana's Kalahari, four villages, over 100 km from the nearest town, cluster together as if for protection and mutual support. Remote as they are, they are of interest to the visitor because so much of the country's early history is represented here. The area may be reached via the Kang–Tsabong route.

Tshane is one of the four villages and it is the old police station which is interesting here. It was built in the early part of this century and is located on high ground overlooking the magnificent Tshane Pan. In addition, the watering of animals from hand-dug wells on the pan's edge provides a fascinating insight into the traditional way of performing this task, which has remained unchanged for 150 years or more.

Lokgwabe, 11 km from Tshane to the south-west, is the home of Hottentot descendants of Simon Cooper, who fought the Germans of South West Africa during the 1904 rebellion. Cooper and his followers sought the protection of Britain and were allowed to settle here. About the same distance north from Tshane is the settlement of Lehututu. Those who are familiar with early explorers of the Kalahari will have heard of this village. Indeed, unlikely as it may seem, it was once a busy commercial centre. Although times have now passed it by, the old store is still standing and remains open for business. Hukuntsi, the fourth village in the group, is the administrative headquarters for the area. Petrol and diesel are sold here and there is a well-stocked store.

TSODILO HILLS (Route 17)

The Tsodilo Hills, located in Botswana's remote north-west, are among the most rewarding of destinations for adventurous visitors. Brought to world attention by Laurens van der Post in his *Lost World of the*

Kalahari, they do indeed speak of myth and mystery and the magic of the place is almost tangible. This is, perhaps, partly because of their setting.

The hills, of micaceous quartzite schists, rise abruptly through rolling sand dune country. The dunes, long since stabilised and held in place now by abundant vegetation, might at first escape your eye, but you will gradually become accustomed to the gentle climb to the 20 m wooded crest and the descent to the flat, grass-covered valley before the next crest.

Four hills make up the group. Set roughly in a line, the most southerly, and the largest, is bare rock, rising 300 m above the plain. Immediately to the north is a group of scattered summits, and beyond that two small, separate hills. The Bushmen call the largest the Male, his companion the Female and the nearest of the small hills, the Child. There is no name for the fourth and smallest hill. It is the Male that is first seen on the approach, its summit looming blue-black above the trees, at once beckoning, and suggesting by its very incongruity and size, the mystery and enigma that is Tsodilo.

There is a permanent settlement of Hambukushu, a Bantu people, near the Male hill. The road will take you to this point and here you will be met by an employee of the Museum who may ask you to sign the visitors' book. No fee is required. Closer to the hill is a small Bushman encampment. There has been Bantu occupation in and around Tsodilo for at least a thousand years and the Bushmen are likely to have made use of it for very much longer. Archaeological studies have suggested occupation by humans for at least 30 000 years. That Tsodilo is a place of special significance to the Bushmen is suggested not only by the existence of a number of secret and permanent springs among the hills, but by the profusion of rock art in the area. There are over 2 700 separate paintings, some of outstanding impact. The majority are on the Female hill and most are to be found around the base on the west and along the side of major drainage lines.

There are no facilities whatsoever at Tsodilo. Food, water and fuel must be taken with you. The nearest fuel is obtainable from Barrie Pryce at Shakawe Fishing Camp, 50 km away. Beyond that, petrol should be found at Etsha 6 village to the south and at Andara in Caprivi to the north. An airstrip at Tsodilo is maintained by the Museum but is not manned. The Bushmen or Hambukushu will act as guides. They will show you a large and convenient cave if you have not provided for yourselves, and can also in emergencies assist with water. An informal curio business exists and vendors will accept payment in cash, although tobacco, salt and beer are highly sought after commodities. A minimum of three full days is recommended to explore the hills fully.

WESTERN WOODLANDS (MASETLHENG PAN) (Route 6A from Routes 3 and 6)

This incredibly beautiful part of Botswana was shown to us by that grand adventurer and man of the bush, Izak Barnard. If you want a first class tour of the area, travel with him but, if you wish to visit independently, we thoroughly recommend a visit.

The pan of Masetlheng lies just 90 km west of Hukuntsi and it is remarkable for four reasons. First, the journey there takes you through a series of striking pans and gives a very good feel of what these features look like (notice the build-up of wind-created dunes on the south or south-west sides of all these pans).

Second, the opportunity of visiting newly founded San villages is illuminating, if somewhat depressing.

Third, is the prospect of still more adventure. This is so because, from Masetlheng, one can explore along existing tracks southwards or to the north-west. The former we have been able to enjoy but the latter remains an exciting prospect, for along that route, towards Ncojane Farms and, ultimately, the border with Namibia at Mamuno, lies Ukwi Pan, said to be the largest in Botswana.

By far the greatest attraction of Masetlheng, however, is the acacia woodland that is to be found just 10 km beyond it. Across a swath of countryside, varying from 3 to 5 km in width and stretching for some 40 km in length (according to Izak) the woodlands consist of a vast stand of large acacias in a field of closely cropped grass.

The dominant trees are *Acacia luderitzii* and *A. erioloba*. There are no young trees and no scrub and so the impression of a carefully manicured and maintained parkland is quite overwhelming. Seen in the late evening with the sun low and the long shadows creeping across the grass between golden trees is striking and unforgettable. It is, I think, one of the most beautiful places I have seen in Botswana. Do go there.

2. HOW TO GET THERE

Having decided which areas in Botswana you wish to visit, this section is intended to help you plan your route. A number of routes are described in great detail. Despite every effort to make it so, however, some of the information concerning the quality of road surfaces will not be accurate. Roads in Botswana change with the seasons, with the amount and type of traffic using them, and depending on how recently a grader has passed over them. The Nata–Maun road is a case in point. On some occasions it is smoother even than tar; on others it is a bone-shaking hell. The Roads Department does the best it can to maintain the roads but its task is monumental and it simply cannot maintain the thousands of kilometres of gravel and sand roads as well as it might wish to do.

A second factor which tends to make the information on road surfaces less reliable than one might desire is caused by the problem of description. What to one person is a fair surface may very well be considered execrable by another. There is no standard by which a convenient measurement can be made. Descriptions used in the following section reflect, as far as possible, what general opinion was at the time when the road was used.

The same subjectiveness also plagues indications of the length of time taken for certain journeys. There are many factors which will influence the speed at which one travels and no two people will do the same journey in the same time. At best, then, we ask you to accept statements of road quality and time taken as an *indication* of what to expect.

If you pride yourself on your ability to get from A to B using maps, logical deductions and by following instructions to the letter, you are in for a new experience in Botswana.

Direction finding in the remoter areas requires boldness, common sense, perseverance and more than a modicum of faith. Even if there were accurate maps, there is absolutely no guarantee that the roads would be the same as they were when the maps were drawn. This is understandable, when you think about it: a herd of elephants passes by, doing its work of tree-demolition. One of the trees falls over the road and the next vehicle to arrive finds its own random way around the obstacle, creating a new road that may only rejoin the previous track many kilometres further on.

Then there are the dreaded sand ridges. Your speed drops, the whine of the engine grows higher and higher as it strains with greater and greater effort. As a last resort, you swing out of the track, hoping to get better purchase on the vegetation alongside. A new road is created.

These facts pose certain problems for the writers of guidebooks who are trying to furnish helpful, clear and concise directions. Our approach is to give you a general description of the lie of the land and approximate direction and distance. You can use the 'decision-point' approach, ie calculate how long it *should* take to reach your destination, knowing how fast you travel and get a feeling for the direction. Drive in that direction for that length of time, keeping a note of times and landmarks. If you haven't arrived at your destination in the time you have allowed, then it is time for a reassessment and maybe a cup of tea or coffee!

SOME COMMON ROUTES FOR TWO- AND FOUR-WHEEL-DRIVE VEHICLES

The route you choose is usually determined by the type of vehicle you are planning to use and by the amount of time available to you.

Two-wheel-drive vehicles

Although kombis have been known to penetrate successfully the heart of the rough country, for the less intrepid explorer the route between Maun and Kasane, through the Moremi Wildlife Reserve via Savuti, is a 'no go' area. However, it is still possible to see both the water world and the big game world of the Delta by following the route below.

Drive Francistown–Nata–Maun. Leave your vehicle in Maun and fly into the Delta. Once there you have a number of options. You can select from a wide range of experiences – from the ultra-luxurious to the basic (and infinitely cheaper) camp and canoe (mokoro). You can find out what is available through local travel agents in Maun.

From Maun, drive back to Nata and from there head north on the tarmac road to Kasane. This is the gateway to the big game world for two-wheel-drive vehicles. You can either camp in the Chobe National Park at Serondela or stay outside the park at Chobe Safari Lodge or Kubu Lodge.

From here you can plan an overnight excursion into Zimbabwe and take the excellent tar road to Victoria Falls. You can continue through Hwange National Park to Bulawayo, then turn south via Beit Bridge. The alternative is to return to Botswana and head south to Francistown.

Four-wheel-drive vehicles (a two-week trip)

If you are approaching the Delta from the south or east, the best route for those short of time is to push through to Maun as quickly as possible. Spend the night there, then refuel, stock up and head northwards to Moremi South Gate. Spend four nights in the Moremi Wildlife Reserve, dividing your time between Third Bridge and Xakanaxa campsites. Then drive north to Savuti and spend a couple of nights there. Head north again to Serondela campsite in Chobe National Park. The final two nights before the journey home can be spent at Victoria Falls.

Once in Maun you will probably be eager to be 'up and at' the big game country and may be reluctant to waste an afternoon wandering among the water-lilies and taking in the phenomenal birdlife of the waterways around Maun. Do take the time, though, to hire a mokoro (dugout canoe) and let your poler take you into this quietness and peace. It is well worth it.

Four-wheel-drive vehicles (a three-week trip)

With more time to spend, all kinds of possibilities are open to the visitor with a four-wheel-drive vehicle. Visits to the Nxai Pan Game Reserve and the Makgadikgadi Game Reserve, especially if your visit coincides with the game migration, are a must.

You can leave your vehicle in Maun and fly into the Delta for two or three days' camping and canoeing. Remember that Maun is the last place where you can hire a mokoro if you follow the Moremi–Savuti–Chobe route.

Begin by taking the standard route through Moremi to Savuti, but thereafter head north to the campsite on the Linyanti River. Alternatively, stop at Tjinga or Nogatsaa, both pleasing, but lesser-known campsites in the Chobe National Park on the route to Serondela.

Caprivi route
Kasane–Ngoma Bridge–Katima Mulilo–Poppa Falls–Mohembo Gate–Shakawe

Nothing in life is all good or all bad. Even war sometimes has a silver lining and in this case it is the road which runs through the Caprivi Strip. This road, which contrasts so strongly with the roads of the Delta, can be used to travel speedily and smoothly from one side of the Delta to the other. The route will be described as though travelling from east to west.

As this route takes you out of Botswana and into Namibia you will have to clear customs. This is done in Kasane as there are no customs facilities at the Ngoma Bridge itself.

Unless you want to do some last minute game viewing along the river bank, take the more southerly main road that leads to Kachikau. It travels along the higher land and then drops down to the river floodplain where the Ngoma Bridge is clearly visible. The bridge will take you across the Botswana/Namibia border. The distance from Kasane to Ngoma Bridge is 64 km and takes about 1 hour.

Your next destination is Katima Mulilo where, after 67 km from the Ngoma Bridge Border Post, you are clearly in a different country. It is a bustling centre and a good place for picking up any spare parts needed or stocking up with excellent Windhoek beer! Note that the South African Rand is the currency used here and South African credit cards are valid.

From Katima Mulilo to the Kwando River is a run of 120 km on a tar road and then there is a good quality dirt road for the remaining 212 km to the Poppa Falls campsite. This appealing campsite is run by the Department of Nature Conservation of Namibia.

There is petrol to be had at Andara – not very far up the road from Poppa Falls – or one can rely on Barrie Pryce having some at Shakawe Fishing Camp, 65 km away in Botswana. Apart from these two sources, the nearest supply will be at Etsha.

At the Poppa Falls campsite you can walk and 'boulder-hop' your way to the main body of water. Looking across its width of about half a kilometre, it is quite a thought that this is the water that becomes the whole of that magical Okavango Delta, 13 000 km^2 of unique wetland paradise.

At the Andara junction, take the road to Botswana. This will take you through the Mhlango Game Reserve to the Mohembo Gate, which is the border between Botswana and Namibia. The distance from the junction to the border is about 35 km.

To clear customs on the Botswana side you will have to go to the police station in Shakawe. From here it is about 15 km to the campsite at the Shakawe Fishing Camp.

DETAILED ROUTES

ROUTE 1: Gaborone-Khutse Game Reserve

Total distance: 220 km. Time: 4-5 hours.

To reach the Khutse Game Reserve from Gaborone, take the tarmac road via Molepolole (51 km and last petrol) to Letlhakeng (about 65 km and end of tar). About 37 km from Molepolole it is worth watching to the eastern side of the road for a striking, deep river gorge. Today the river no longer flows but the incised nature of the valley and its precipitous cliffs indicate the huge volumes of water there must once have been.

From Letlhakeng the road is poorly signposted. It is sandy and particularly so some 20 km beyond Khudumelapye (about 23 km) and on the approach to Salajwe (about 39 km). The Khutse gate is 44 km beyond this last village.

ROUTE 2: Gaborone-Mabuasehube Game Reserve

Total distance: 533 km. Time: 11 hours.

There are three approaches to this reserve. One is from the south, through Tshabong. A second route is from the north, via Kang and Tshane. (For details of these routes see Route 6, Kang-Tshabong.) The third route, which approaches from the east, is considered to be the best and is recommended - the road is better and the distance shorter.

To travel by this route, drive from Gaborone to Khakhea, via Lobatse and Kanye, Jwaneng and Sekoma. (For details of this section see Route 3, Gaborone-Ghanzi, and Route 4, Jwaneng-Werda for details of the Sekoma-Khakhea section.) From Khakhea drive south on the main road to Werda for approximately 55 km. Keep your eyes open for an unmarked turning to the right 1,5-2 km before the crossing of a noticeable dry river bed, which is the Moselebe. The river itself is approximately

25 km from Werda and 55 km from Khakhea. More explicit directions are not possible because, since the writers were last on this road, it has been completely re-aligned and tarmac has been laid down.

The distance from Khakhea to Werda has been increased by 10–15 km as the new road is much further to the west than the old. This is because its purpose, as a rural road, is to connect villages, not necessarily to provide the shortest distance from one place to another.

We can only emphasise the idea of working backwards from the Moselebe River and we are confident that the cut-line will rejoin the new road as people will certainly continue to use this handy route to Mabuasehube.

Once located, there remain only 143 km of perfectly straight track with no corrugations and very little sand. You will be driving through the very heart of typical Kalahari country.

ROUTE 3: Gaborone–Ghanzi

Total distance: 731 km. Time: 12 hours.

The road to Ghanzi from eastern Botswana is long and arduous. There is only one practical route and a four-wheel-drive vehicle is most certainly recommended. The journey can be done in an ordinary vehicle but this could be asking for trouble.

Starting from Gaborone, drive 75 km south to Lobatse. From Lobatse continue south for 5 km, then turn right at the well-signposted junction for Kanye (45 km) and Jwaneng (a further 75 km after Kanye). At Jwaneng, the site of one of Botswana's diamond mines, you are 200 km from Gaborone, all of which has been on full-width tarred surface.

From Jwaneng, proceed directly over the first traffic circle you come to. There are 2 or 3 km of tar before the 85 km of gravel road to Sekoma. The gravel can at times be corrugated and hard; at others the surface is fairly good. There is a track which runs parallel to the main road on the south side. This is slower, and sometimes quite sandy, but it does provide an alternative. If you look carefully you will soon become adept at identifying those places where the locals, knowing the road well, leave it for a side track and later return to it again, avoiding particularly rough sections.

Shortly before Sekoma there is a fork in the road, the left branch of which takes you to the southern Kalahari. Continue straight after Sekoma, and you will arrive at Kang after passing through Mabutsane and Morwamosu. Both villages have small general dealers and bottle-stores. Water is also available there. From Sekoma to Kang it is 161 km. Average speeds will vary with the time of year and amount of traffic that has been using the road. You are unlikely to do better than 50–60 km/h.

In the vicinity of Mabutsane the road can be very sandy and throughout the distance to Kang the surface may be exceedingly irregular. However, it is used daily by many vehicles and is by no means impassable.

Kang is one of the largest villages on the route. There are several stores here, including a butchery and a bottle-store. Fuel is also available but be warned that the prices are the highest in Botswana. You will be able to get fuel after normal shopping hours in certain circumstances. The road forks at Kang, the left branch turning south to Tshane and Tshabong. Continue straight on.

From this point the road surface deteriorates still further. There are short sections of gravel and calcrete, whilst the remainder is sand. Deep ruts will be encountered, so be vigilant and drive with care. There will be little evidence of habitation between this point and Ghanzi itself as all the villages are set somewhat off the road. For this reason it is a good idea to keep a log of your journey, noting turn-offs, villages passed and distances covered. In the event of some emergency it may help to know in which direction it is best to go for assistance.

There are many boreholes along this route, although set back from the road. They are part of the chain that was established for watering cattle being trekked from Ghanzi to the abattoir at Lobatse. None is signposted.

Takatshwaane, 155 km north-west of Kang, is most easily identified by the dry river bed you will cross and by the Roads Department camp on the left-hand side of the road. The village accommodates many Bushmen who have settled in the area. A further 30 km beyond Takatshwaane brings you to the crossing of the Okwa River. Flowing only in years of exceptional flood, and then only for short periods, the river is nevertheless of interest. It was once a major tributary of a great lake that covered as much as 80 000 km^2 of northern Botswana. A glance at the high banks and great width of the river valley is enough to confirm the former size of this now ephemeral river.

From Takatshwaane to Ghanzi is 125 km. Ghanzi offers a full range of facilities. There is a small hotel, which makes arrangements for campers, and there are shops supplying most general goods. There is also a hospital and radio-telephone contact with the rest of the country.

ROUTE 4: Jwaneng–Sekoma–Khakhea–Werda

Total distance: 211 km. Time: 4 hours.

(For directions to Sekoma, see Route 3, Gaborone–Ghanzi.)

A four-wheel-drive vehicle is recommended because, until the new road (see below) is finally completed, there will always be sections possibly impassable to ordinary vehicles. At the time of writing, Jwaneng remains the last fuelling station until you reach Werda.

At Sekoma, there is a tarmac turn-off to the south. For this surprising and welcome sight we must thank the people of Norway who are paying for 160 km of new road. The completed tar now runs from Sekoma through Khakhea and, at the time of writing, was just 10–15 km short of Werda. From there the road will turn south-westwards, along the border to the village of Makopong. There it will join an existing length of tarmac which reaches to Tshabong.

You will find two sets of parallel tracks and most people keep to these. Sometimes the centre section is quite hard and wide enough for a vehicle, and here the going is easier, although it is difficult to get onto it. It is a reality of Kalahari roads that people often drive on the 'wrong' side of the road. Thus one needs to be particularly alert for oncoming vehicles. Overtaking requires more time and care than you might ordinarily use.

Follow the road south from Khakhea, which can be identified by the very large pan to its immediate west.

There remain 80 km to Werda where you may purchase both petrol and diesel and there is a general dealer who stocks most items you are likely to need. It is possible to leave Botswana at this point. To do this, report to the Botswana Police who serve as immigration authorities. There is no corresponding facility on the South African side and so you are required to travel to Bray, 58 km away, and report to the South African Police there. Border facilities are available from 8 am to 4 pm only.

ROUTE 5: Werda–Bokspits

Total distance: in Botswana – 381 km. Time: 9 hours.
via South Africa – 457 km. Time: 8 hours.

A four-wheel-drive vehicle is not required on this section.

To reach Werda, either enter Botswana from Bray, in the Republic of South Africa, or see Route 3, Gaborone–Ghanzi and Route 4, Jwaneng–Werda.

The distance from Werda to Tshabong is 136 km. The first 59 km are on good, firm sand and no difficulties will be encountered. A cruising speed of 70 km/h can be comfortably maintained. From the 59 km post and the village of Makopong, a good tar road goes to Tshabong, which has most basic facilities for the visitor.

The section from Werda to Makopong is the subject of a current road building programme, funded by the people of Norway, which is tarring the road from Sekoma to Makopong via Khakhea and Werda.

There are two ways to get to Bokspits from Tshabong. One lies inside Botswana and the other in South Africa. The former is not recommended. It is 110 km to Khuis and a further 135 km from there to Bokspits. The road is used daily but is extremely badly corrugated. Progress will be slow and uncomfortable and there is no fuel along this route.

To leave Botswana at this point, it is necessary to report to the police at Tshabong before departing. Take the good gravel road south for 26 km to McCarthysrust, the South Africa border post, which is open from 8 am to 4 pm. From McCarthysrust to Vanzylsrust is 132 km on excellent, signposted, gravel roads. Vanzylsrust offers all the usual facilities. From there to Bokspits is a further 163 km on similar, good quality roads.

It is worth deviating, however, at a point 11 km west of Vanzylsrust. Here there is a signposted turn-off to the right which takes you to the South African border post of Middelpits 26 km away, and beyond it, in Botswana, a group of villages on the banks of the Molopo River.

The Molopo River, now dry except for occasional and short-lived floods, was a great river in times gone by, as is evidenced by the massive valley and the eroded calcrete walls. Worthy of a visit are the high cliffs just below the village of Khuis and the impressive gorge, carved through solid rock, at Kolonkwaneng. Both villages are within a radius of 10 km from Middelpits. There are no Botswana border requirements. Very basic supplies are available in the village stores.

Whilst travelling from Vanzylsrust to Bokspits you will follow the Kuruman River which takes its name from the amazing spring at the town of Kuruman. In this area, however, the river seldom flows.

The entry into Bokspits is well signposted. Shortly before the border is a motel, close to which you will see the turning for South African customs, open only from 8 am until 4 pm. Visitors entering Botswana are required to report their arrival to the police at Bokspits. Fuel and basic supplies for the independent traveller can be purchased in Bokspits.

ROUTE 6: Kang-Tshabong

Total distance: 344 km. Time: 10-11 hours.
(For directions to Kang from Gaborone see Route 3, Gaborone-Ghanzi.)
A four-wheel-drive vehicle is necessary for this journey.

The first section consists of 104 km from Kang to Tshane, on a sand road with no gravel. The sand can be quite soft and deep in places. Fuel is obtainable at Kang and also at Hukuntsi, which is 11 km from Tshane.

There are several points of interest along the way to Tshane, the first being a settlement of Bushmen, or Basarwa as they are known in Setswana, at a place called Letlhake, on the roadside 47 km from Kang. A further 17 km along this road brings you to a second, similar settlement, known as Kgainyane. Zaatshoni Pan lies 7 km further on, and provides an opportunity to see one of these unusual features at close quarters.

Tshane is one of four villages which cluster together in the heart of the Kalahari. (For more detail see Where to Go: Tshane/Hukuntsi Cluster of Villages.) It is 240 km from Tshane to Tshabong. The dirt road is very badly corrugated and traffic volume is light. You will be obliged to drive slowly and the journey is uncomfortable, taking up to 8 hours. There are no towns, villages or facilities along the way, although water may be available from the ranger stationed at Mabuasehube Game Reserve. His camp will be found high up on the north-eastern side of the only pan you actually drive across, near the 130 km point.

Beyond this pan there are a further 110 km of bad road, which can take up to four hours, before Tshabong is reached.

ROUTE 6A: Hukuntsi-Western Woodlands (Masetlheng Pan)

Total distance: 100 km. Time: 4-8 hours.
(For directions to Tshane and Hukuntsi, see Routes 3 and 6)
A four-wheel-drive vehicle is necessary for this journey.

In Hukuntsi, ask the way to Masetlheng Pan – it will be extremely difficult to find otherwise. The village is a maze of unmarked tracks, and without guidance and in the absence of any signs a guide or at least directions are highly recommended.

Once found, the road is followed out of the village first to the west, later it swings to the north-west. The track will be sandy and difficult for it was along this cutline-line that Perto-Canada dragged their massive drilling rigs when, in search of oil in 1989/90, they drilled a 4,1 km borehole at Masetlheng Pan.

A pan called Kwakai will be the first feature encountered. This is just before the large Zonye Pan, which is 28–30 km from Hukuntsi. The road is deep, soft sand and the going is extremely slow.

After Zonye Pan, 7 km further on and some 33 to 35 km out of Hukuntsi, is Bohelabatho Pan. A further 3 km beyond that, Bohelabatwana Pan will be encountered.

The scenery then returns to that of the essential Kalahari until 73 km from start have been covered. Here one should cross Ngwaatle Pan. On the far side of this feature and only a kilometre or two from it will be found a San village.

There still remain 28 km to Masetlheng Pan. When the pan is reached, proceed a further 10 km along the track and take your pick of the wonderful campsites which abound in the woodlands to the north-west of the pan.

ROUTE 7: Serowe–Orapa

Total distance: 212 km. Time: 2¼ hours.

Since this guide was first published, this road has been tarred and nearly four hours taken off the journey!

The turn-off at Serowe is a few kilometres before the town centre but is well signposted. There is no pertol along the route, except at Letlhakane, at its northern end.

Now that drivers will have time to look about them as they travel to Orapa, there are several features worth noticing.

Between Serowe and Paje you will notice an escarpment to the west. This is the edge of the Kalahari. The flat-topped hills about you are outliers that have been left behind by the westward moving effects of erosion.

After the sharp left-hand bend at Paje the road begins to climb the escarpment and basalt boulders appear on both sides. This basalt, exactly the same system as that which creates the Drakensberg, underlies the Kalahari sands at this point. On the edges of the road, as you reach the crest, the familiar red sand of the Kalahari is first seen.

After Paje, the next village is Mmashoro, where you will see a flat-topped hill on either side of the road. You might be amazed to learn that on each summit there are extensive, important and extremely old Early Iron Age sites. Evidently, the Kalahari has not always been seen as inhospitable.

Between Mmashoro and Letlhakane, you will be stopped at the Makoba veterinary fence. (From this point, if you intended to travel up the east side of Sowa Pan, you would proceed north, along the fence on a good track to Tlalamabele on the Francistown–Orapa Road.)

As you approach Letlhakane, you will see the massive dump of the mine away to the north. This is DK1, the mine itself, not the village, which you encounter from about 189 km onwards.

The handiest petrol is at 191,5 km among some shops on the left-hand side of the road. At this point there is also a T-junction to the right which eventually leads on 12 km of excellent gravel road, to the main Francistown–Orapa road at a point exactly opposite the track to Kubu Island, one of the access routes for Sowa Pan.

For Orapa, do not turn right but continue straight on. The road leads you to the east gate of the mine at 212 km.

The diamond-mining town of Orapa is contained within a large security fence. It is private property and permission is needed to enter. Whilst the town has all facilities, they are not automatically available to the general public. A permit may be applied for, in advance, from the head office of Debswana in Gaborone (PO Box 329, Gaborone. Tel 351131, Fax 352941). Alternatively, you could try to persuade the security personnel at the guarded gates to let you in, but you will not necessarily be successful. Emergencies will, of course, be treated sympathetically. The main road by-passes Orapa to the south (21 km) and leads on from there to Mopipi Reservoir and the Boteti River.

ROUTE 7A: Mopipi–Deception Valley

Total distance: 153 km. Time 4–5 hours.
A four-wheel-drive vehicle is essential.
Route 7 takes one from Serowe to Orapa Mine. To get to Mopipi, the starting point of Route 7A, drive 21 km around the south side of the

Orapa Mine Concession and a further 46 km from the point at which you rejoin the main road, westwards to Mopipi.

From the petrol station at Mopipi Village, find a track off the road back to Orapa that circles Mopipi Reservoir on its east and south side. (The Reservoir is that vast, circular grey, dry and dusty area before you – usually quite empty of any trace of water!) After some 9 km you will reach a junction where a road departs from the 'circular drive' and heads off to the south-west. Take this road.

In the next 30 km you will pass, on your right-hand side, Lake Xau – where once, when it had water, wildebeest used to herd in their thousands – then drive through the Kedia Hills, past a smaller pan on your right and then, at a cattle post 40 km from Mopipi petrol station, you will turn due west onto a cutline.

After 29 km you will encounter a new veterinary fence that cuts diagonally across in front of you. Follow the fence 20 km to your right. Firstly you will travel in a north-westerly direction and then, after curving to the left, to the west and finally south-west. The fence ends as it reaches the Central Kalahari Game Reserve boundary.

It is necessary at this point to follow the boundary 6 km to the north-west to reach the game scouts' tented camp. The scouts may or may not be present (at the time of writing it was only a temporary camp). If the scouts are present park entry fees will have to be paid (see page 95).

Once entry formalities have been attended to, an 8 km drive to the south-west will take you back onto the east–west cutline you were originally following before being diverted by the veterinary fence. You rejoin it at a 'crosstracks'. Straight on (south) will lead you to a San settlement after 70 km whilst right (west) will take you to Deception Valley.

After a total of 44 km west along the cutline you will drive onto Springbok Pan. Just beyond it is Deception Valley and some 10 km from the eastern edge of Springbok Pan you will encounter a track to the north which leads, after only 3 km, to Sunday Pans.

(We are indebted to Mr Noel Strugnell, Chairman of the Orapa Bush Club, for assistance with these directions.)

ROUTE 7B: Ntwetwe Pan

Route 7B (1): Orapa to Gweta
Total distance: 129 km. Time 4–5 hours.
(To get to Orapa see Route 7)
A four-wheel-drive vehicle or LDV is recommended.

To pass through the mine concession area of Orapa is only possible if a permit has been obtained by prior arrangement with Debswana, Box 329, Gaborone. Tel 351131, Fax 352941. Permits are not lightly granted.

On reaching the east gate the mine area can be bypassed by following the (usually poor) dirt road round to the south of the concession area. A journey of 21 km will bring you back onto the Orapa–Mopipi road some 3 km west of the west gate. It is at this point that the route to Gweta begins.

Drive directly north, across the main road, and continue in this direction. To begin with, the mine perimeter fence will be on your right. Soon, this fence turns abruptly to the east and the road diagonals to the north-west. Follow it for a total distance of approximately 36 km from the start.

Having travelled through rather unattractive scrub lands, on roads of very indifferent quality, you will have noticed the increasing occurrence of vast grasslands, interspersed with woodland.

After 36 km you will come to the banks of the Boteti River where it cuts through the base of the great tongue of land that juts into Ntwetwe from the south. North of this point are prairie-like grasslands of great beauty. They and reaches of accompanying woodlands extend over a further 30 km to the north, which will bring you to a new veterinary fence and the edge of Ntwetwe pan.

The next 20 km over the pan is very fast going but care and common sense are required if the surface is wet. If, due to water, you cannot see the spoor of a vehicle in front of you, do not go on unless you are very sure of what you are doing. This track is heavily used by people commuting from Orapa to Gweta and if there is no spoor, you are either in the wrong place or the way is impassable.

Approximately 10 km north onto the pan surface will bring you to the island of Gabasadi. It is difficult to recognise for the first time, being nothing more than a low sandy prominence of your left-hand side (west). A further 20 km beyond Gabasadi you reach the Gweta mainland.

Travelling north and about 3 km from the edge of the pan you will see a turn-off to the east. After 5,4 km along this track you will reach Chapman's Baobab. Continuing north past this turn-off for 10,5 km will bring you to Green's Baobab. From this tree to the village of Gweta is 25,5 km.

If one is attempting the journey in the reverse direction seek the assistance of villagers at Gweta to get onto the correct track. A mistake can be enormously frustrating and, in the absence of signs, is easy to make.

Route 7B (2): The Western Islands

A safe route to the western islands is to turn west at the point where the north–south track reaches the Gweta mainland. Careful observation may show you the spoor of previous travellers in this area but from this point on, a map is best relied upon.

A general, but not very helpful picture of the region can be obtained from the 1:250 000 "Bushman Pits" monochrome map. However, for navigating through the islands and the areas referred to in this text, you should have the 1:50 000 series maps 2024 D2, D4, 2025 C1, C2, C3 and 2025 A4.

Some of these are full colour and therefore P6.50 each. Others are black and white photographic mosaics and cost P3.50 each. They can be obtained from the Department of Surveys and Lands, P/Bag 0037, Gaborone, Botswana, Tel 353251.

These we consider the minimum to navigate successfully. Your own experiences and individual requirements must be relied upon if you want a wider spread. Any competent geographer will be able to help you plot these maps out onto the 1:250 000 so that you can see those areas covered in detail.

Route 7B (3): Nata–Maun road to Gabasadi Island

Total distance (approximately) 75 km. Time 2–3 hours.

A different and interesting route into this area is from the Nata–Maun road. At a point of 51 km from Nata the north-east 'finger' of Ntwetwe crosses that main road and it is easy to get down onto the pan surface. It is not so easy to drive south-west 'down' the finger. The exercise is fun but requires some directional skill, a lot of common sense and some luck too.

We have seen heavily laden vehicles sink throuth the surface – but escape with relative ease. However, driving with care can avoid these calamities.

Large areas of grass make it difficult to find a clear 'open pan' surface, especially in the northern reaches. Eventually, however, patience is rewarded and an excellent route will be found by staying close to the western shore of the 'finger'. This can be followed round to the south to meet up with the Gabasadi road.

On the journey along the 'finger', you will encounter a track coming out of the open pan and running from south-east to north-west. (You can turn north-west along this track to Gweta, south-east to Kubu Island, or continue south-west along the present shoreline.)

This track is a last, but also scenic and exciting, route into the area. It is most easily described from the Kubu Island turn-off (see Route 8(2)).

Route 7B (4): Kubu Island to Gweta
Total distance: (approximately) 100 km. Time: 3–4 hours.
From the Kubu turn-off, travel north. After 8,4 km you will pass a low (now dying) acacia tree on the left with a small borrow pit (formed by the extraction of road-building material) on the right. After 12,4 km you will reach the pan edge where the bush begins again. There is a turning to the west 1,5 km beyond this with two or three huts in evidence. A further 2,3 km north brings you to a second turning to the west. This is the start of the track to Gweta. Set your odometer to zero here.

To ensure that you have the correct turn-off, verify that there is a single baobab in sight on the west side of the road and that the track passes between it and a group of huts on the right with an acacia tree growing inside a wooden pallisade surrounding the huts.

After following this track to the north-west for 9,4 km you arrive at another new veterinary fence. At 21 km the open grasslands are reached and in this vicinity are two beautiful acacias which will make a wonderful photograph for whoever gets to them at the right time of the day. At 38,1 km there is a fork in the road: take the left side. By some 50 km from the start you will find yourself driving on part of the Ntwetwe Pan surface but the road returns to the mainland again before crossing the 'finger' at approximately 65 km, making a further 35 km to Gweta.

ROUTE 8: Sowa Pan

Route 8 (1): East of Sowa Pan
A four-wheel-drive vehicle is not essential for this route.
There is a little-known track, maintained by Botswana's Veterinary Department, that runs near the east side of Sowa Pan and gives excellent access to the area.

The southern end of this track begins on the Francistown–Orapa road at Tlalamabele and the cordon fence (approximately 150 km from Francistown). There is a barrier across the main road which is manned 24 hours a day. Approaching from Francistown, the track you seek begins on your right-hand side, immediately before the barrier. Ask the guard to open the gate for you.

Once onto the track, which follows the double fence in a northerly direction, the going, although a little rocky in places, is on a firm, smooth surface. As you drop down, off the escarpment, you will be driving occasionally on the edge of the pan. This can be slippery when wet. After 50 km you will reach a manned gate. This is the turn-off to Kukonje Island (see Where To Go: Sowa Pan). From here it is only 47 km, on an excellent track, to the tarred Francistown–Nata road. You emerge at the Dukwe veterinary gate, on the south side, approximately 130 km from Francistown.

About 15 km towards Nata from the Dukwe gate is a signposted turning to the left labelled SUA. This will take you to what is known as the Sowa Spit – a long tongue of land that juts far out into Sowa Pan. It is approximately 40 km to the base of the spit and the site of Botswana's Soda Ash Project. An additional 18 km will take you along the spit to its western extremity. All the roads on this section are either good gravel or firm sand.

From the base of the spit you will find a track going north-east. This breaks up into a maze of smaller tracks which will deliver you either to the main road again or to Nata, depending on your luck and sense of direction! Much of the travelling in the latter part of the journey is on the pan surface. Providing you are following other tracks and the surface is not wet, you will experience no difficulties. After heavy rain this particular area is quite impassable.

Returning to the main Nata road, at a point 20 km from Nata there is a prominent baobab tree on the left-hand side of the road. Beside it is an unlocked gate in the fence. The track that begins here leads a short way down to the edge of the pan. You can either 'guesstimate' your way to Nata or go back on the route by which you came.

Route 8(2): West of Sowa Pan

This section can be travelled in an ordinary vehicle but a four-wheel-drive is strongly recommended. This is because of the greater loads that must be carried and because of the additional flexibility it allows.

The starting point for this section is at Nata. (For directions to Nata see Route 9, Francistown–Maun. Note: there is a difficulty with all the following directions for the west side of Sowa Pan. A new road is being built from Nata to Maun. It will not necessarily follow exactly the course of the present road. You will have to use common sense in interpreting these directions after the new road is complete.)

There are two main routes down the west side of Sowa Pan. One follows a series of tracks down the dry (and very dusty) mainland between the two pans; the other is along the edge of the pan surface.

Dealing with the latter first, one starts at Sua Filling Station at Nata and takes the dirt road to Maun. After 10,3 km there is a track to the left (south) opposite a grass-covered mound on the north side of the road. Turn left here and meander south through the grasslands for 9,7 km. Whenever there is a fork in the road, always choose the southerly alternative. We recall a particularly difficult junction to find on a sharp bend.

If you've been lucky and found the right tracks you will find yourself on the pan surface at some spoil dumps we call the Pyramids suggested by the shape of the spoil dumped when the trench was dug. The trench is part of the exploration for what is now the Sowa Pan Soda Ash project which extracts salt and soda ash from the sub-surface saline brine. Do stop and examine the strange aquatic life that is growing there and that assumes such grotesque and repulsive forms. But treat it with great responsibility for it is a scientific phenomenon which is not yet understood. Current experiments at Cambridge University will, hopefully, soon tell us more about it.

The next section is not for the faint-hearted. From the Pyramids, you must now rely on your sense of direction and common sense. The island of Kubu lies 81 km to the south, across the open pan. Stay close to the shore and good luck – it is an exhilarating drive!

A less exciting but safer alternative route is to continue westward on the track you selected at the 10,6 km mark, ignoring the Pyramids and the open pan choice. This track will lead you to the route down the mainland between the two pans.

If you miss the 10,6 km track there are others at 16 km and near the 18 km mark. At this last mark is a large baobab and beside it a track to the south. Any of these tracks will do; they all lead south between the pans. The track is firm, but in places exceptionally dusty. It is a fine, black dust which once formed the old lake bed on which you are travelling.

The object, on this section, is to maintain a southerly direction. The tracks will separate and join again and again. If anything, make a deliberate error to the east. You'll always recognise Sowa Pan when you see it!

After 64 km you will pass the village of Thabatshukubu. It is not signposted, nor has it any facilities (it is little more than a large cattle post) but it is distinctive in being perched on a very low ridge. From its vicinity you'll have your first clear view of Sowa Pan to the east.

The road is less difficult to follow from this point on. About 33 km to the south is the turning east to Kubu Island. The exact position of this turning is extremely difficult to describe as the area is quite featureless. It is, however, on the actual pan surface, at a point where the road runs across it. The turning itself is marked by a pile of stones on the east side of the track and, if you are on the lookout for it, is not difficult to see. A clue will probably be other vehicles' tracks leaving the road and heading off in a north-easterly direction, through the tussocks of grass in the distance. One further clue, when approaching from the north, is a stunted acacia thorn tree on the west side of the road. Opposite is a low grass-covered mound. This is an old gravel heap, just over a metre in height. The tree has, unfortunately, succumbed to drought and appeared dead when we last passed that way. If this is so, it will probaby not be left standing for very much longer before becoming firewood. The tree and the mound are 8,4 km north of the Kubu turn-off.

There is now a veterinary fence across the north–south road on which you are travelling. The gate in this fence is exactly 6 km south of the Kubu turn-off and 21,8 km north of Mmatshumo village.

Between the village and the fence is a distinctive line of trees across which the road passes. This point is 16 km from the Kubu junction.

Travelling south from the pan the road climbs steadily up a low escarpment. If you are observant you'll be able to distinguish the various shorelines and at one place, where the road is quite rocky, you will be driving across an old, rolled pebble beach. This is the worst section of the road. The lake bed deposits are particularly fine and deep ruts have been worn in the track. Many alternative tracks have been created and it is wise to make use of them for they avoid the worst places. If you are in an ordinary vehicle, it is here that you will have the most trouble. In any vehicle when this section is wet you can expect to have difficulty. The village of Mmatshumo has a small general dealer and a bottlestore.

Route 8 (3): South of Sowa Pan

From Mmatshumo it is 22,7 km to the main Orapa–Francistown road. This road is reached directly opposite the point where a first-class gravel road leads 12 km south to join the Orapa–Serowe road at Letlhakane village (see route 7). The intersection is a major one and difficult to mistake. It is 18 km west to Orapa's East Gate and you are approximately 212 km from Francistown. Of this distance to Francistown, in January 1991 only 70 km remained untarred.

An alternative route is to travel east from Mmatshumo for 48 km on a passable dirt road to the village of Mosu. Near this village one needs to be wary of the many gullies that cross the road. From Mosu it is a further 27 km to the veterinary fence on the main Francistown–Orapa road at Tlalamabele.

ROUTE 9: Francistown–Maun

Total distance: 495 km. Time: 5 hours.

Starting at Francistown, travel north-west along the main tarred road towards Kazangula. There are two veterinary fences to pass through before reaching Nata at 187 km from Francistown. The first of these, the Dukwe fence, will be found at 130 km; the second (a new fence) is at 167 km.

The turn-off to Botswana's Soda Ash Project, at Sowa Pan, is signposted to the west at 140,5 km from Francistown.

At a point 170 km from the start you will see the large baobab tree on the west side of the road mentioned in Route 8 (1). A few kilometres beyond this tree is Nata Lodge, a haven for long-distance travellers 178 km from Francistown or 9,1 km out of Nata.

It is at Nata that one leaves the tar and begins the 304 km journey to Maun. This is the last petrol station before Gweta, 100 km further west. Nata is also a good place to fill up with water, now that its water supply problems have been solved.

(Note: there is a difficulty with all the following directions for a new road is being built from Nata to Maun. It will not necessarily follow exactly the course of the present road. You will have to use common sense in interpreting these directions after the new road is complete.)

The dirt road from Nata to Maun is usually of a fair standard. Certainly there is no need for a four-wheel-drive vehicle. Occasionally, short sections become badly corrugated but this is generally nearer the

Nata end and in the vicinity of the Makgadikgadi Pans. At the 99 km post is a signposted left turn to Gweta where there is water, a general dealer, a safari camp and a bottle-store. It is also an access point for the Makgadikgadi Pans and grasslands.

At 59 km from Maun you will be stopped at the Makalamabedi veterinary fence where the gate is manned 24 hours a day. Nothing is required of you here except to provide information on where you have come from and are going to. Your vehicle registration number will be recorded. If you have a dog with you, you must produce a veterinary permit authorising its movement about the country.

All facilities are available in Maun – good shops, fuel, health services, international communications, hotels and camping grounds.

ROUTE 10: Makgadikgadi Game Reserve from Nata-Maun Road

Total distance: approximately 110 km. Time: 2½–3½ hours.

(Note: there is a dificulty with all the following directions for Makgadikgadi Game Reserve. A new road is being built from Nata to Maun. It will not necessarily follow exactly the course of the present road. You will have to use common sense in interpreting these directions after the new road is complete.)

A major north–south route begins in the north at a turn-off opposite the game scouts camp on the main Natu–Maun road. This camp is located on the north side of the road (next to a Roads Department camp) among a grove of large acacias and is approximately 39 km west of Gweta or 137 km west of Nata. Maun is some 168 km further to the west.

Visitors intending to enter Makgadikgadi Game Reserve are expected to pay the fees required and to do so at this point. This is difficult to achieve for visitors from the south or east and, at the time of writing, the problem had not been overcome. It is believed that a southern entry point may be built in the future – but where or when cannot presently be said.

The entrance to the game reserve is opposite the game scouts camp. Beside the gate is a painted map board and it is recommended that visitors note down the details shown thereon.

The old north entrance road, mentioned in previous editions of this guide, has been closed, although vehicles have taken to driving round the trench dug to stop vehicle movement.

To traverse the game reserve from north to south, begin at the game scouts camp and enter the reserve there. (A turn-off after a few hundred metres goes a short distance to an artificial water-hole – well worth spending a few hours at.)

Travel 14 km south-west. At that point there is a T-junction (unsignposted) to your left. Turn left, and after a further 5,3 km (during which the sharp-eyed among you will notice Njuca Hills looming above the scrub to the south-east) you will reach a second T-junction. Turn right here and travel south-west and south for about 16 km. This should bring you to a third turn-off to the left (south). Take this turn-off and drive due south along a cutline for 43 km. On the way you will pass Nomad Pan and will see why it is so named. At the end of that distance will be another turn to the left. Take this and, after some 27–33 km (depending on which of the many tracks you follow southwards) you will reach the tarmac between Mopipi and Rakops. Turn left for Mopipi.

Approaching this route from the south one needs to be aware of the several sharp right angle bends – which particularly confound the night-time motorist – encountered when travelling west, soon after the petrol station at Mopipi has been left behind. At 19,1 km a track to the right (north) will be discerned. It is not signposted. There is a rusty metal post on the left-hand side of the road – but bare of any sign. Opposite is a well-worn track. Beside the track is a pile of calcrete but the distinctly white feature of which we once wrote is no more. You will simply have to look carefully.

Taking this track to the north you will drive for 27 km through exceedingly dusty and braided roads, eventually emerging onto the grasslands with some 80 km of good driving ahead of you.

To get to Xhumaga from the game scouts camp on the Nata–Maun road, enter the reserve at the main gate and drive for 48 km in a south-westerly direction without taking any side roads.

To reach Njuca Hills, a number of routes are possible. Two will be described, starting from the game scouts camp on the main road.

Enter the reserve and travel 14 km south-west along the Xhumaga road. At that point there is a T-junction (unsignposted) to your left. Turn left. After a further 5,3 km (during which you may notice Njuca Hills just visible above the scrub in the south-east) you will reach a second T-junction. Turn left for 2,7 km to the first of two tracks that take you up onto the back of the dune and a superb campsite.

To return to the main road from Njuca via a different route drive east from the hills for 10,6 km. This will bring you to a distinct group of palm trees, known as Makolwane a ga Wateka, and what appears to be a T-junction with one track continuing to the east (it goes 50 km to Gweta but it is not a very good track) and another turning north. Take the last-mentioned which, after 11,5 km, will deliver you to the main road. Turn left (west) and, after 3 km, you will be back at the game scouts camp.

ROUTE 11: Nxai Pan from Nata–Maun road and Baines' Baobabs

Total distance: 35 km. Time 45 minutes to 1¼ hour.

(Note: there is a difficulty with all the following directions for Nxai Pan and Baines' Baobabs. A new road is being built from Nata to Maun. It will not necessarily follow exactly the course of the present road. You will have to use common sense in interpreting these directions after the new road is complete.)

The turn-off to this park is to be found on the main Nata–Maun road and is approximately 170 km from Nata or 135 km from Maun.

A sandy track leads north from the main road. After 17,4 km you will come to a crossroads which is the old Nata–Maun road. It is also the turn-off for Baines' Baobabs. Drive straight on for a further 17,5 km to reach the entrance gate of Nxai Pan National Park.

The vicinity of Baines' Baobabs has become popular since this guidebook was first written – the fact that the area is outside the now expensive National Park may have something to do with this.

More extensive use has increased the number of (informal) campsites now available. Almost all the great baobabs along the shore of the pan have a cleared space where a good site may be found.

There are two recommended routes to the area of these famous and very beautiful baobabs. The choice is dependent upon the direction from which you are approaching since the discovery of much shorter routes may save considerable time and mileage.

If you are approaching from the west, use the Nxai Pan turn-off from the main road and proceed to the first crossroads at 17,5 km as described. From this point, turn right for 0,9 km to a fork in the road. You can go either left or right at this fork but the latter is recommended.

The road leads 11 km directly to the baobabs on a fair surface. The alternative route is longer (17 km, and requires that you know where to make a right turn after 13,3 km), less comfortable, but vital for the wet season when the shorter route may be flooded or too wet for safe travel.

If you are approaching from the east it is possible to save some 35 km in distance and about an hour in time. The critical point ,when travelling west from Nata, is to find your turn-off to the north 133 km from Nata. This turn-off has several features which identify it.

At the junction itself is a small metal sign, on the north-west corner of the intersection, which is marked BTC/Nera Site No 22. Opposite this, on the south side of the road, is a large and overgrown borrow-pit (created by the extraction of road-making material). At 1,5 km beyond the junction (to the west) and on the left-hand side of the road, is an unmarked track emerging from Makgadikgadi Game Reserve (see Route 10 – it comes from the group of palm trees). Beyond that and a total of 4,5 km from the sought-after intersection, is the Makgadikgadi game scouts camp.

Two turnings to the left will be seen; one after 2 km and a second after a total of 5 km. At the first turn-off a double line of fences will be seen on the right-hand side of the road, marking the corner of a large Government experimental cattle ranch. Ignore both this and the second turning.

At 10,1 km from the main road a third turning to the left will be encountered. Turn left here. After 4,3 km a well-marked track to the south will be seen. We have not explored this but suspect that it leads either to the Post Office telecommunications tower or to the Roads Department camp. Ignore the turning and continue for a further 13,5 km. This will bring you into the grasslands 3,6 km from and within sight of Baines' Baobabs. From this point the track is very unclear and you need to use your common sense to reach your final objective.

Leaving the trees and going east by this route is possible but not easy – again because the track (at the time of writing) was very difficult to pick up. If you want to try it, this is what we did: Starting from the centre of the camp site at the trees, go north for 1,6 km along the standard northerly exit track. Look for a very faint track to the right, off the road on which you are travelling. Turn east along it for 0,7 km, then north-east onto the exit track which soon swings east and becomes well marked.

ROUTE 12: Maun–Ghanzi

Total distance: 280 km. Time: 4–5 hours.
Much of this section is dirt road of variable standard, but a four-wheel-drive vehicle is not required. From Maun, set off in a southerly direction

along the tarmac main street. The 65 km of road to Toteng (and beyond to Sehitwa) is presently being tarred. Parts of the road are badly corrugated and pot-holes are occasionally encountered. Average speeds of 60–70 km/h can be maintained.

At the small village of Toteng there is a clearly signposted left turn to Ghanzi. From here the road is alternatively sandy in patches or hard calcrete, which can be both very corrugated and deeply pot-holed. Generally, the surface is adequate and an average speed of 50–60 km/h is possible. There is a veterinary fence at Kuke, 98 km from Toteng. It is manned 24 hours a day and only basic information is asked by the attendant. A permit is required if you have a dog with you.

Once through the Kuke gate you enter the Ghanzi farming area. After 79 km you will come to the small farming village of D'kar. There is a well-stocked store here and plans are currently being made to sell fuel here too.

Ghanzi is 38 km beyond D'kar.

ROUTE 13: Ghanzi–Mamuno

Total distance: 210 km. Time: 4–5 hours.

This journey can be done in a saloon vehicle and four-wheel-drive is not necessary although we must warn you that the road surface is enormously variable. The first 60 km of road from Ghanzi are in poor condition. The surface is calcrete which is hard and unyielding. It is both corrugated and covered with pot-holes. After this section, as the calcrete ridge of Ghanzi is left behind, the road becomes sand which is firm and offers a comfortable ride all the way to Kalkfontein, 113 km from Ghanzi. From this point to the border at Mamuno, a distance of 96 km, the road is again calcrete with corrugations and deep pot-holes but it is not as bad as the earlier section.

If you are planning to travel between Ghanzi and Windhoek, the total distance is approximately 575 km and you should allow 9 or 10 hours for the journey.

ROUTE 14: Maun–Lake Ngami

Total distance: about 90 km. Time: 1–2 hours.

There are two approaches to the lake, one from the north and the other from the south. Both involve travelling from Maun to Toteng, a distance of 65 km, currently being tarred, as described in Route 12. At this village there is a road to the left which crosses the Lake River and turns southwest towards Ghanzi. From this road, or by going straight past Toteng, you can gain access to the lake flats. There are no signposted roads to the lake shore but in either case it is as well to travel about 15 km from Toteng before turning into the bush to explore whatever track you find. Some 4 km short of Sehitwa (about 25 km from Toteng) on the left-hand side is a signposted turning to a fishing camp which indicates that fish are for sale. Owing to the ephemeral nature of the lake, the sign is somewhat misleading! It does, however, offer easy access to the immediate vicinity of the lake shore.

ROUTE 15: Maun-Drotsky's Cave

Total distance: 315 km. Time: 9-11 hours.

The easiest route by which to reach the caves is from Maun, via Sehitwa and Tsao. The 98 km from Maun, presently a fairly rough calcrete road, is being tarred. At the end of 1990, 19 km of the section from Maun to Toteng had been completed and it is expected that the full distance to Toteng (65 km) will be ready by the end of 1991. Work will then begin on the remaining section of 33 km to Sehitwa.

The 43 km from Sehitwa to Tsao has been tarrred for some years now and this section has since been extended.

At about 1,5 km past the turning (north-east) to the village of Tsao you will see a turn-off to the left. This used to be marked with a signpost, bearing the zebra logo of Botswana's museum and the legend 'Drotsky's Cave'. When we were last there the sign had been knocked over. Although we re-erected it, it may have fallen over once more. So keep a sharp lookout! From this point the road is sand for 146 km until the next turning. A four-wheel-drive vehicle is essential.

The first two-thirds of this portion pass through wooded, undulating, sand country, without any distinct pattern in the low dunes. This area was once flooded and part of the Okavango. Later you will come upon more distinct and larger fossil dunes. They mark the furthest reaches of the once far more extensive delta. From here the sand is very heavy and the going slow. The 146 km from Tsao will take you 5-6 hours. After crossing a particularly sandy dune, look out for a magnificent view over to the west. About 30 km away to the north-west you will see the Aha Hills. On the downhill slope there is a second signpost, again with the zebra emblem, pointing to the left, and a bush track which follows the river valley 26 km to Drotsky's Cave.

ROUTE 16: Drotsky's Cave–Aha Hills

Total distance: 47 km. Time: 2 hours.

The Aha Hills can only be reached from the main Maun–Shakawe road. The easiest route is to turn off at the Drotsky's Cave signpost, just north of the village of Tsao. (For details of the first section, see Route 15: Maun–Drotsky's Cave.)

From the signpost 26 km from Drotsky's Cave the village of Xai Xai is approximately 11 km. From this village the road turns north to the hills 10 km away. It is possible to return via Dobe, in which case continue north, past the hills, for about 60 km. At that point you will come to a T-junction. Turn west and drive 20 km to Dobe or east and travel directly to Nokaneng. The 172 km to Nokaneng is exceptionally difficult. The road is deep sand for which a four-wheel-drive vehicle is a necessity. This route is not signposted.

ROUTE 17: Maun–Tsodilo

Total distance: 355 km. Time: 9–11 hours.

There are two approaches to Tsodilo, both of which lead from the main Maun–Shakawe road to the west of the Delta. A four-wheel-drive vehicle is essential.

From Maun to the nearest turn-off at Sepupa is a distance of 310 km. The route to Sepupa is undergoing dramatic changes. As you will have read (Route 15) much road construciton is taking place between Maun and Sehitwa. The same is true to the north-west of Tsao.

For some years now there has been a (welcome, but isolated) 43 km stretch of tar between Sehitwa and Tsao. This has now been extended so that in December 1990 it reached past Nokaneng and Gumare to Etsha. Construction is still in progress and it is hoped that the road will, in due course, stretch to Sepopoa and perhaps even Shakawe.

Beyond the tar, before you reach the southern turn-off near Sepupa, the road surface will deteriorate and you will find stretches of very deep, loose sand. A few kilometres before Sepupa, after crossing a dry river bed, you will see a sign on the left-hand side of the road indicating the road to Tsodilo. The sign carries the zebra logo of Botswana's museum.

There now remain about 45 km to the hills. The first part of the journey is on a firm bush track. It is advisable to remove, or fold in, wing mirrors. Just after halfway you will encounter dune country. The valley floors are hard and driving is easy, but the route lies diagonally across the trend of dunes and a number of them must be crossed. The sand on the dunes can be very thick and loose. The total time from Maun will be between 9 and 11 hours, and from the Sepupa turn-off to the hills approximately two and a half to three hours.

The alternative route to Tsodilo is via Shakawe. The turn-off to the hills is approximately 8 km south of the village and, as previously, it is signposted. The hills form the third point of an equilateral triangle between Shakawe and Sepupa. Going via Shakawe, therefore, is taking a longer route by about 50 km. However, the road is slightly better, the sand is not so deep and Shakawe, situated on the high banks of the Okavango at the beginning of the panhandle, is worth a visit. The village has a clinic, a store and radio contact with Maun – and fuel is sold by Barrie Pryce who runs a fishing camp at Shakawe and does cater for casual visitors (see Chapter 7).

ROUTE 18: Maun–Moremi–Savuti

Total distance:
(By-passing Moremi): 197 km
(Direct via Moremi): 245 km
(Including grand tour of Moremi): 335 km

Total time:
5– 6 hours
6–10 hours

Some people manage this route in an ordinary vehicle but this is not recommended. There are no facilities for the general public along this route, but water is obtainable. There is no fuel. For directions to Maun, see Route 9, Francistown–Maun.

All the roads in this section are sand except for a tarred stretch between Maun and Shorobe. After this point the surface is mostly sand or clay which, in places, can be very slippery when wet. Crossing Mababe Depression, when the 'black-cotton' soil there is wet, is extremely difficult.

Travel north-east from Maun along the Thamalakane River. It does not matter which side of the river you are on. If it is the west side, you will arrive at the Matlapaneng Bridge, a few kilometres outside the town. If you cross the river by the Francistown road bridge, turn north immediately after doing so.

From Maun it is 3 km to the first major village of Shorobe. One third of the way there the road forks. There is no signpost. The left-hand fork is the scenic drive, closer to the river. Both roads go to the same place. Generally, the scenic drive is very deep, loose sand and not at all to be recommended, especially as there is little to see. It is better to stay on the tar. At 5,4 km before Shorobe the scenic road rejoins the main road. At Shorobe there are several small general dealers and it is often possible to purchase locally woven baskets, some of which are of a very high standard.

Beyond Shorobe, and 9 km from it, is a fork in the road. Although the left fork leads to the south gate of Moremi, the road is exceptionally sandy and the going slow. Continue straight for 19 km to a signposted junction to the left.

The left turn leads to Moremi 'South Gate' (29 km). Continuing north allows you to by-pass Moremi Wildlife Reserve and continue straight to Savuti (132 km). This route is recommended for those who are trying their luck with a two-wheel-drive vehicle as it avoids the difficult crossing of Magwikhwe Sand Ridge.

If you choose to pass through Moremi you will arrive at the manned South Gate with its public campsite. An entrance fee is expected for vehicles, passengers and camping, if you plan to spend a night in the reserve. The gate opens at dawn and closes at dusk.

From South Gate, there are two routes. The first is a drive around the Moremi peninsula to the North Gate. Mboma (30 km) is the western extremity. On the return journey you will come to Third Bridge (about 7 km) and Xakanaxa (about 13 km).

At the latter there are a number of private camps and a public campsite. From Xakanaxa it is a further 50 km to North Gate, where there is another public campsite. The alternative route is to travel from South Gate directly to North Gate (30 km), crossing a wooden bridge over the River Khwai just before the exit.

From North Gate the road turns east for 38 km and joins up with the main road from Maun to Savuti. Approximately 20 km from North Gate you will come to the Magwikhwe Sand Ridge. This fascinating feature (which can best be seen in the vicinity of Savuti) is a relic barrier beach from the days of Botswana's super-lake. Its summit stands at the highest level ever reached by the lake. However, the immediate problem is to cross it. Four-wheel-drive is definitely needed. The sand is especially deep and soft as one crosses the ridge. Beyond it the road descends to the hard surface of Mababe Depression and no further problems should be encountered. It is approximately 25 km from the eastern foot of the ridge to the park boundary.

The South Gate of Chobe National Park (also manned from dawn to dusk) is 58 km from Savuti. An entrance fee must be paid, as for Moremi. The only official camping place is at the public campsite on the banks of the Savuti Channel.

ROUTE 19: Savuti–Kasane

Total distance: 207 km. Total time: 6–8 hours.

There are two routes from Savuti and the Mababe Depression northwards, towards Kasane. Most people take the more westerly one, which, although it is the shortest in distance, is by far the most difficult and takes much longer in time.

A better route from Savuti is to go eastwards via Ngwezumba Dam. Not only do you see more of the park and, at certain times of the year, very much more game, but the sand road is often good, particularly after rain, and invariably better than the deep loose sand of the western route. However, *be warned*, the nature of roads in this part of the world is exceedingly variable; *always expect the worst*.

To follow this route, start at the crossing of the Savuti Channel itself and take the main road north, past the signposted turning to Linyanti, for 3,1 km. You will have just crossed an old and faintly discernible river channel. At this point turn right to what is known as Harvey's Pan. Either route east from here leads you towards Quarry Hill, which you can see clearly from the Pan. Pass this immediately on your left, still going east.

At the 30 km point, ie from where you turned off to Harvey's Pan, another road joins yours from the right and your direction now begins to swing increasingly north-east. Within 20 km, you will start to follow the dry bed of the Ngwezumba River. After a further 83 km you will reach a signposted junction. Turn right into the complex of roads around Ngwezumba Dam, the public campsite and Nogatsaa.

To get to Kasane by the most direct route, do not turn right here but continue straight on. After 22 km you will come to a second intersection. This also allows access to Nogatsaa and the campsite. Continue straight for 36 km until you arrive at Nantanga Pans, 1 km beyond which is the main road from Kasane to Ngoma Bridge. Turn right for Kasane (32 km) or continue straight to reach the Chobe River (10 km).

Botswana distance chart

Distance table in km

The distance of the most direct route is shown in the chart. Measurements have been taken from the best available sources and all are subject to 5% error.

From \ To	Bokspits	Francistown	Gaborone	Ghanzi	Jwaneng	Kang	Kanye	Kasane	Kazangula	Lobatse	Mahalapye	Maun	Nata	Orapa	Palapye	Ramatlabama	Ramokgwebana	Selebi-Phikwe	Serowe	Serule	Tshabong	Werda
Bokspits		1156 via Werda 874	433		519																	
Francistown	1156 via Werda 874			202 via Kang 712	274	240	319															
Werda	724	433																				
Sekoma 591	629	via Maun 778	519		82 via Fwn 1122	via Gweta 1152	via Fwn 1029															
645	via Lobatse 871	202 via Kang 712	274	240	82	via Gweta 1152	via Fwn 1029															
Gweta 1755	547	120	592		via Fwn 1122	via Gweta 1245	via Fwn 1035	via Gweta 1041														
Gweta 1747	488	via Fwn 909	via Gweta 933		via Fwn 1109		via Fwn 741		12													
649	480	via Fwn 921	via Gweta 920	637	127	363	45	1008	996	273												
921	508	75		via Maun 1013	400	636	318	735 via Nata 616	723 via Nata 604	via Fwn 990	717	via Gweta 304										
Ghanzi 1151	235	198	286	801		via Ghanzi 865	via Fwn 1035	312	300	via Fwn 690	417	via Fwn 724	420									
Gweta 1455	492	915		817		via Lobatse 1110	741	via Fwn 732	via Fwn 720	748	475		351	403								
1397	188	via Fwn 621		864		via Lobatse 708	792	663	651	345	72	655	744	796	393							
1000	240	673	1010	471			390			48	321	via Fwn 1048	270	322	380	638						
Lobatse 697	163	270	via Maun 941			411	93	1056	1044													
1239	556	123	via Lobatse 685	175		953	635	582	via Fwn 570	590	317	574	339	391	132	525	233					
Palapye 1134	82	515	via Maun 860	711		840	522	651	639	477	204	643	398	450	47	432	292	179				
1046	151	402	via Maun 929	605		via Lobatse 747	429	709	697	384	111	702	279	324	72	465	164	60	119			
1046	210	315	via Fwn 988	517			462	585	572	417	144	583		1151	748	451	993	888	800	828		
246	84	342	via Maun 869	545		via Lobatse 780	399	1411	1399	410	676	via Ghanzi 905	1099	1017	620	323	865	754	666	693	128	
381	910	478	619	via Sekoma 333		345	283	1283	1271	275	548	777	965									
777	350	491	198	217																		

3. FACTORS AFFECTING YOUR CHOICE

SEASONS AND CLIMATE

Botswana is a huge country, roughly the size of France, and extends through nine degrees of latitude. This fact alone suggests considerable variation in climate. It is also landlocked and very nearly in the centre of the Southern African subcontinent, on an elevated plateau of approximately 1 000 m. These factors tend towards low annual rainfall.

The seasons in Botswana are indistinct. Rains generally start in October or November and persist through to March and April. Within that period, however, there may be long dry spells. With the cessation of rain in April, temperatures begin to fall and May is generally regarded as the first month of the dry, cool winter, characterised by clear sunny days and cold nights. Frost are over by August and temperatures rise rapidly during the hot, dry period of September, October and November until the rains break again.

Although the rainy season is generally from October to April, there is great variation in the time of its arrival and departure, in the quantity of rain that falls and in its distribution. The quantity of rainfall decreases from the north-east of the country to the south-west, and as it does so its variability increases. Thus the wet north-east might expect 600 mm of rain with a variability of about 30 per cent, whilst the drier south-west will receive, on average, only 200 mm, with a variability of about 80 per cent!

Generally speaking, rain tends to fall in short, sometimes violent thundershowers. Although rain may first fall in September, it is generally true to say that the greatest amount falls in the months of December, January and February.

Temperatures can be quite extreme in Botswana, with the greatest range occurring in the south. The following table shows the mean maximum and minimum temperatures, in °C, in four months of the year at five locations in Botswana.

	April	July	Nov	Jan
Kasane	30/15	25/8	33/19	30/19
Maun	30/15	26/6	34/20	30/19
Francistown	28/14	24/5	32/18	31/18
Gaborone	28/12	22/2	32/16	32/18
Tshabong	28/11	22/1	33/16	35/19

It is important to realise that these figures are only averages and that actual maximums and minimums can be very different. For example, there have been several reports of snow in the Kalahari and it is not uncommon for small quantities of water to freeze solid overnight in winter. On the other hand, maximum temperatures, especially in the hot months of October and November, can sometimes reach 40°C or more.

BEST TIMES TO VISIT THE PARKS AND RESERVES

Botswana's national parks and game reserves have their own particular attractions at any time of the year. However, if your specific objective is to see game and to witness the great migratory herds, the following guide indicates the best times to visit.

Chobe National Park

(a) The river front at Kasane and Linyanti.
Good all year round but best from May to October.

(b) Inland and the Savuti area.
From November to May, although, if the Savuti Channel is flooded or water remains throughout the year in the Mababe Depression, May to October also offers excellent viewing.

Moremi Game Reserve

Viewing here can be good all year round but the dry season months from May to November are usually best.

Okavango Delta

The Okavango is a vast wetland, the size of which varies through the year, being controlled largely by the rains which fall in Angola and which are transported to it along the Okavango River. The floods arrive at Mohembo, at the north-western end of the Delta, as early as December, building up to a peak between January and March, but occasionally as late as May. These same floods slowly work their way through the vastness of the Delta in the succeeding months so that the highest levels in Maun, at the opposite end of the Delta, are not recorded until July or August or sometimes in September. The Delta is at its largest during the months of June and July and at its minimum extent in December and January. Although fishing can be good throughout the year, the best months seem to be from August to February, whilst the best game-viewing months are from July to October.

Nxai Pan National Park

Successful game viewing in this national park depends very much upon whether or not rain has fallen. If the rains have been good, December to early April are excellent months. If they have failed, a visit to the park can be very disappointing from the point of view of seeing game.

Makgadikgadi Game Reserve

From June onwards, until the first rains fall in late September or October, the grasslands become increasingly occupied by herds of migrating antelope and their attendant predators.

Central Kalahari Game Reserve

This reserve is now open to the public. Having existed since the sixties as a pristine sanctuary set aside for the exclusive use of the San it has been, intentionally, completely undeveloped.

Recent changes, therefore, require a new approach and it will take time for roads, tracks, campsites and official entry points to be established.

Until all this is in place, visitors who decide to explore the reserve must be prepared to make payment of normal fees if game scouts are encountered or if they enter either through Khutse or by the Deception Valley route.

It is unlikely that the Department of Wildlife National Parks would wish to encourage visitors to the reserve at the present time.

The drought has severely reduced many of Botswana's game species and too much must not be expected of this reserve. As with Khutse several good rain years need to have elapsed before we can hope for the return of game in substantial numbers.

Khutse Game Reserve

It is unusual to see significant quantities of game in this reserve, particularly of late owing to the prolonged drought. There need to have been several good years of rain before the game is likely to return in large numbers. Khutse is renowned for its excellent birdlife.

Mannyelanong Game Reserve

At this nesting colony of Cape vultures the birds are best seen in the winter months, from May to August or September.

Mabuasehube Game Reserve

The largest concentrations of game will be seen in the vicinity of these pans during the rainy season from October through to April.

Kalahari Gemsbok National Park

The park is divided by two major rivers, the Auob and the Nossob. Game viewing is always good, one reason for the park being open all year round. However, along the Auob, from June to October, it is particularly good. The same is true for the Nossob from January until April. It is well worth paying a visit to the great dune-fields that stretch between the two rivers during the rainy months. Covered with lush vegetation, they make a most striking sight.

CHILDREN IN THE BUSH

Parents should think very carefully about taking younger children on holiday to the wildlife areas of Botswana. Apart from the long and often uncomfortable distances to be travelled, there is an element of danger.

Public campsites in the National Parks are unfenced and there are no facilities where little children can play unattended, so constant watchfulness on the part of adults is required.

Operators refuse children under 12 and reluctantly accept children over 12, but there are no reduced rates for children. This is not so with Botswana's National Parks and game reserves. In this case children of 8 years and below are allowed entry free and there is a reduced rate for those between 8 and 16 years of age. See Park Entry Fees and Regulations on page 95.

Traveller's tale: Savuti campsite is situated next to the Savuti channel which for the past few years has been quite dry. Some 50 m across the channel from one of the camping places is the skeleton of a crashed aircraft.

The ruin was an instant drawcard to the four children who had just arrived. With parents engrossed in setting up camp, the four bounded straight to the plane, exploring it and playing round it.

The underground water and the trees of Savuti channel are a constant attraction for thirsty elephants who are regular visitors to the area.

The inevitable happened and the children and a young bull elephant were in the same place at the same time. By the time that parents and children emerged from their busy oblivion, the elephant's looming bulk separated the two groups. The romance of the wild was suddenly a very frightening and threatening reality for the inexperienced city dwellers.

Fortunately, sheer fright froze all movement but the emotions and adrenalin were almost tangible. Perhaps that was what made the elephant quietly move on and away, averting a potentially very nasty situation.

BIRDLIFE: WHERE AND WHEN

At all times of the year there is an abundance of birds to be seen in Botswana, although in the colder months, between April and September, there are fewer birds around. During that time mostly resident birds will be seen, only a few winter visitors and no European migrants. The warmer months, therefore, are best for bird-watching.

Another factor that strongly influences the number and species of birds is the presence or absence of water. In a dry area there will be fewer birds; the same applies to a poor rainy season.

There are seasonal concentrations of birds in Botswana but they are difficult to predict. For example, at Lake Ngami very little will be seen if the lake is dry. If it has water in it, however, it is one of the most prolific bird localities in Africa. The same can be said of the salt pans in Botswana. The birdlife is very rich if there is water, but if there is none, a visit can be disappointing. This is particularly so of Makgadikgadi Pans, especially north-eastern Sowa Pan. Here, if there is water towards the end of the rainy season, millions of birds congregate, notably flamingos, pelicans and ducks. Yet if there is no flooding, relatively few birds will be seen.

Good areas for the keen bird-watcher are the Chobe, the Okavango and the Limpopo valley. An experienced bird-watcher may expect to see up to 200 species in a week at the Chobe or in the Okavango, among them possibly slatey egrets, shoebills and wattled cranes. In the Limpopo valley, it would not be surprising to see 150 species in the same period of time. In a dry part of the Kalahari, Mabuasehube for example, one might expect to see only 30 to 50 species of bird.

Botswana does boast one or two birds of particular interest to the specialist. The south-east is one of the only two localities in Southern Africa where the short-clawed lark occurs. In Ngamiland the black-faced babbler has been sighted. The only other place where this bird is found is Namibia.

There is a bird club in Gaborone which leads regular walks from the National Museum on the first Sunday of every month, starting at 6.30 am in the summer and 7.15 am in the winter. The secretary and committee are always delighted to assist visiting bird enthusiasts in any way they can. They can be contacted at P O Box 71, Gaborone.

FISHING: WHERE AND WHEN

There are three primary fishing areas in Botswana – along the Chobe River, in the Okavango Delta, and the Limpopo valley in the east. Much of the better fishing in the Limpopo is on private land and so not easily accessible to the visitor.

In the two other areas tiger fishing can take place throughout the year but is generally at its best from August to February, when the water is low, although the annual flood can sometimes produce some excellent sport. The best time to fish for bream and tilapia is also in these months. Barbel can be caught at all times of the year but, like others, low water levels give the best chance of success.

It is difficult to give more precise information about the best months for fishing, especially in the Okavango. Much depends upon what part of the Delta one is visiting. The size and time of the flood has a major effect upon the quality of fishing and, as it varies greatly in volume and in time of arrival, and as it can take five to six months to work its way through the entire system, there are a number of variables which will affect your choice. Having decided on a fishing holiday, the best course of action is to contact some of the fishing camps mentioned in this guide and ask their advice.

Trees and other snags on the bottom of the rivers and channels will lay a heavy claim to your line, spoons and hooks. It is advisable, therefore, to have a large supply on hand. Steel trace and swivels are essential if it is tiger fish you are after. Do remember that crocodile and hippo still abound in large numbers, particularly in the Okavango and in the Chobe. It is foolish to take unnecessary risks.

4. PREPARING FOR THE TRIP

Although there is no real substitute for experience, it should not be necessary for people making their first safari into the wilds, especially the wilds of Botswana, to have to 're-invent the wheel'. This section aims to provide some useful information so that you will be suitably prepared and equipped for a safari. There is nothing more frustrating, when you have arrived at a point 200 km from nowhere, than finding that the salt, toilet paper, tin-opener or film for the camera have been forgotten!

Ultimately, what you carry on safari is your personal choice and what is suggested below should be regarded simply as a guideline. The experienced traveller may find little of use here but those who have not safaried extensively may well find this section helpful.

There are a few basic 'golden rules' worth keeping in mind:
1. Keep everything simple – you have come to see and enjoy, to get a break from home, not to take it with you. There is many an abandoned vehicle on the sides of Botswana's roads that collapsed and died from overweight!
2. Never leave a water point without filling all your water containers. You can allow roughly 5 litres of water per person per day as a guide for provisioning. This does not include an allowance for washing.
3. Never leave a filling station without replenishing your petrol or diesel – you may always meet somebody else who needs it in an emergency.

WHAT TO TAKE

Accessories

If wildlife, birds, the stars or endless vistas are what you are interested in, binoculars are an absolute must. So, too, is a camera. For larger game a 200 mm lens is recommended and for birds, a lens of a minimum 400 mm is necessary. A wide-angle lens of 35 mm or less is helpful in doing justice to the magnificent views. A word of warning about optical equipment. Prodigious quantities of sand and dust are synonymous with the Kalahari and Botswana. Take the greatest care, therefore, to protect delicate equipment. You will need considerable ingenuity and effort to be successful in this regard – merely carrying your equipment in its container or a cloth bag is not enough. The dust will get in. Some people carry cameras and binoculars inside sealed plastic bags – and they also carry a spare supply of plastic bags. Professional photographers never wipe dust from a lens. Instead, dust should be blown off with compressed air, small canisters of which can be obtained from photographic shops.

Hats, sunburn creams (especially the barrier type) and sunglasses are essential, particularly if you are not used to the heat and the glare – both of which can be formidable. Insects can be a nuisance and repellents are recommended. Don't forget Chloroquin anti-malaria tablets (recommended for Botswana).

Some people regard a compass as a panacea to all problems of navigation. In Botswana this is certainly not the case unless (a) you know where you are to start with, (b) you have maps of the area you are in, (c) you know how to use a map and compass and (d) you can work by dead-reckoning (because there are very few landmarks to help you).

Clothing

During the day, throughout the year, a shirt or blouse and shorts or a light skirt are all that are really necessary. A pair of jeans or slacks, a long-sleeved cotton shirt and swimming costumes are all useful items of clothing on safari. A jersey or jacket is handy for the winter mornings. A useful combination is a warm hat or balaclava and a sleeveless waistcoat or jersey. If your head and chest are warm, the rest of your body feels warm. Dun colours are generally more suitable as they attract less attention and, it is said, do not draw tsetse-fly to them as readily as do brighter colours. White is not really a practical colour. Clothes should be of a hardy and durable material – washing of clothes may not be possible as frequently as one might wish and thorns are a constant menace to delicate fabrics.

For night-time during the summer months, day wear is quite sufficient. In winter, however, especially from May to August, it can get very cold at night, so cold in fact that a small canister of water may freeze solid. A change of warm clothing is therefore highly recommended. For the same reason, campers should have warm sleeping-bags. Track-suits are useful as they help to build up layers of insulation as the temperature drops, and they are comfortable for sleeping in. Winter also suggests warm socks, gloves and a hat, cap or balaclava, especially for those a little thin on top!

Shoes

There are as many opinions as to the correct footwear for the Kalahari as there are makes and types of shoe. The choice is yours, but these guidelines may help you. It is not recommended that visitors go barefoot. The sand can get too hot to walk on and your feet can actually blister. Thorns, insects and scorpions are other hazards. Heavy boots are a matter of choice but something lighter is really more practical. Choose a shoe which can be easily removed (so that the sand can be emptied out!) and which is made of a porous material, something that is easy to wash and which allows the foot to breathe. Open sandals, tackies or running shoes are all suitable. A pair of 'flip-flops' is handy for use around the camp.

HEALTH PRECAUTIONS

Diseases

Malaria, a disease transmitted by infected mosquitoes, is encountered in all parts of Botswana and visitors are urged to take anti-malaria tablets. The type of malaria most commonly encountered is Falciparum, one of the complications of which is cerebral malaria, which can be a very serious condition indeed. Generally speaking, the malarial threat is worst in the northern part of the country. In this area you are advised to take anti-malaria tablets throughout the year.

There are two major schools of thought concerning the problem of malaria. You either kill off the tiny one-celled beasties (the prophylactic route) or you use cunning and devious means to dissuade the mosquitoes from coming anywhere near you in the first place.

On one tour there were two couples espousing both approaches and we watched with interest to see the outcome. A naturopath couple believed that foreign substances, like prophylactic drugs, should not pollute their bodies, so they followed the 'repel the mosquito' option. This involved consuming, every hour, on the hour, one clove of garlic.

In complete contrast, the other couple not only swilled their anti-malaria tablets but also copious draughts of whisky, and smoked foul-smelling cigarettes and cigars.

It was the hottest time of a sweaty, steamy summer and the miasma of garlic around our naturopaths was almost visible. It had also been a good season for mosquitoes. Conditions for the experiment were ideal. As the tour progressed, it became apparent that things weren't working out as anticipated. The mosquitoes left one of the whisky-swigging smokers strictly alone, focused a concerted attack on one of the garlic eaters and were ambivalent about the remaining whisky and garlic partners.

Moral of the tale: don't place your faith in garlic, alcohol or tobacco alone and stay up-wind of them all. You could, of course, take the approach adopted by many of the locals – just get on with business as usual, ignoring the prophylactics because they are not 100 per cent guaranteed against malaria and could mask the symptoms, a more dangerous situation as the infection might not be correctly diagnosed. You must make your own choice – but do be very aware that malaria is prevalent in Botswana.

Visitors who have come from a non-malarial region should not expose themselves to unnecessary risks and should take a prophylactic. Botswana medical authorities recommend the following:

Two weeks before arrival in the country, a double dose of two Chloroquin tablets. Two on the first day, two on the second, followed by two a week thereafter and for six weeks after the visit. Doses should be suitably reduced for children. Chloroquin is effective against cerebral malaria varieties.

Despite the common occurrence elsewhere in Africa of the phenomenon, there is no evidence in Botswana that resistant strains of malaria are developing.

AIDS is present in Botswana and routine precautions against contracting the HIV virus are no less important here than anywhere else. There is no need to go to the extent of bringing your own needles in case of accident or emergency, although some people certainly do. Doctors, hospitals and clinics are well versed on the, now, standard anti-AIDS procedures. We have witnessed the use of new needles and watched the destruction of used equipment in a hospital.

Bilharzia is an ever-present threat in Africa, and Botswana, despite its desert-like reputation, is no exception. As a general rule, it is probably safe to assume that all rivers, streams and dams are infected, although not heavily. This is also true of the Okavango, especially around populated areas. The only way to avoid contracting the disease is to avoid bathing or wading in water. Curiously, bilharzia cannot be caught by drinking untreated, infected water. Saliva is sufficient to prevent contamination. The disease is easily cured today. Symptoms take at least six weeks to develop.

Trypanosomiasis, or **sleeping sickness**, a disease transmitted by the bite of an infected tsetse-fly, is a very much reduced threat in modern Botswana. At its widest extent it occurs only in Ngamiland, in the area of Ngami, Okavango, Mababe and Chobe. Today it has been virtually eliminated and only small populations of tsetse-fly exist. The fly can inflict a painful bite and, if you should contract the disease, its symptoms develop only after approximately two weeks. They include headaches and a fever. A blood test can quickly confirm if a patient is suffering from sleeping sickness. The condition is easily cured.

Rabies is endemic among many animals in Botswana. Its occurrence is often marked by cases of unusual behaviour, which may include attacking humans. In the case of a bite from a suspected rabid creature, it is important to get the patient to a hospital as soon as possible. A vaccine is available which requires only five injections and which is extremely effective, if administered quickly enough after the bite. There is no prophylactic which can be taken for protection.

Tick-bite fever commonly affects many people, especially newcomers to the country and, therefore, visitors. It is prevalent in the wet season, particularly in March and April and is passed on to humans from the bite of a tiny, pin-head size tick. The disease incubates for seven days and then manifests itself with severe aching of the bones, headaches, backaches and a fever. Although it can be serious and exceedingly unpleasant, it is a self-limiting disease and will run its course in three to four days. Typically, the symptoms include swollen and painful glands. Almost always an infected bite will be found – it will have a yellow head with a small black central spot. There is much controversy as to whether immunity can be acquired by stoically enduring the pain until the body's system defeats the infection. Medical advice in Botswana recommends that there is no merit in following this questionable course and suggests instead that the sufferer should report to a hospital where the disease is easily controlled through a course of tetracycline.

Finding ticks on your body is an experience you might have to get used to. They are, however, easily dislodged but care should be taken that the head as well as the body is removed, or infection might result. Removing very small ticks can be a problem. A useful way is to smear them with vaseline, grease or a commercial sealant. A drop on the tick causes it to release its hold and it can be pulled away when the sealant is removed.

Venoms

Scorpions are numerous in the sandveld of the Kalahari but care can be taken to avoid them. Simple precautions include shaking out clothes and emptying out shoes before putting them on. The unwary are often bitten while picking up firewood, and it is best to kick or knock the wood before picking it up. Many scorpions live in trees, especially under loose bark. A sting can be extremely painful but it is not generally dangerous. Within an hour or so, the effects will have worn off. The best treatment is to cool the site of the sting and to administer mild pain-killers, if available.

Dealing with the question of **snakebite** is a difficult issue. Broad spectrum anti-snakebite serums are available and you should consider taking one with you. Generally they have a short shelf-life and need to be kept constantly cool, if not refrigerated. This is not always easy to achieve. Sometimes, it has been claimed, an anti-venom injection has caused more problems than it has cured. You need to know your snakes and how to use the serum if you are going to carry it.

An alternative to a snakebite kit is a new method of treating snakebite which, to us, is a far more attractive choice. Known as the Sutherland Method (after its Australian originator) or the Pressure Immobilisation System, it requires only a few crepe bandages.

It is not the intention here to explain the system in full but, essentially, it requires that the victim be rested, soothed and relaxed. The injured limb is completely bound – from one end to the other – with crepe bandages using firm but gentle pressure. The idea is to restrict the movement of the lymph system in which the poison is transported. NO TOURNIQUET IS APPLIED.

An advantage of the system is that, in contrast to the tourniquet method, which can dangerously stop or hinder blood flow, the affected limb is not at risk on that account.

Wolf Haacke, snake expert at the Transvaal Museum, who is an exponent of the method, tells us that more about it can be learnt from Johan Marais's book *Snake versus Man* and from most snake parks.

Our recommendation is to study this method as it seems a sensible and hopeful compromise between risking the dangers of incorrectly administered serum and doing nothing at all.

Other

It is recommended for those who wish to take sensible precautions, that visitors consider having a hepatitis A and B **vaccination** before entering the country. An alternative is an injection of immune globulin which will prevent contracting this common disease for about three months. It is also advisable to have a tetanus and a typhoid booster.

Venereal infections are quite common, especially gonorrhoea.

Water in the towns and villages is perfectly safe to drink.

The **sun** in the Kalahari is fierce and those whose skins are not used to it should wear hats and should apply sunburn creams, especially the kind with ultra-violet screening properties. The **dust** in the dry season will irritate eyes which are not accustomed to it so take eye-wash solution with you. Mild attacks of **diarrhoea** are not uncommon, for which Lomotil, a non-prescription medicine, is an effective cure.

There are general **hospitals** at the following locations: Maun, Ghanzi, Gaborone, Francistown, Lobatse, Mahalapye, Serowe, Selebi-Phikwe, Molepolole, Kanye, Mmadinare, Mochudi, Ramotswa, Jwaneng and Orapa.

Many of the villages throughout the country have **medical clinics** staffed by trained personnel. These clinics should be regarded as a resource not to be overlooked, especially when assistance is needed for less serious complaints. Many are in radio contact with hospitals.

First aid

If you intend to travel independently, and to the remoter areas, take a first aid hand-book with you. Many lives have been lost unnecessarily through failure to take the simple precautions clearly outlined in such a book. In addition, you should carry a first aid kit – the Automobile Association, the Red Cross or any chemist will help you select suitable items for it.

Heat-stroke may prove to be a problem and your first aid equipment should include salt tablets. Some people may find that the intensely dry air of the Kalahari causes congestion in the sinuses and, for this reason, a decongestant of some kind should also be included.

Infection can spread very rapidly so keeping clean on safari is important. It is possible, with practice, to complete a respectable bath with only three mugs of water! Sweat-rashes often result from a combination of dirt and heat. Talcum powder will control this condition but cleanliness will help avoid it. Another aid to controlling infection is a styptic pencil. Rubbed on those annoying bites, it reduces the irritation – and hence the scratching – thus lessening the chance of infection from dirty finger-nails.

VEHICLE SPARES

Always carry at least one spare wheel, a jack and wheel brace. A puncture repair outfit is of no use without tyre levers and both are a good idea to carry. Essential spares include fuses, tyre pump, tyre pressure gauge, light bulbs, points, condensers, spark plugs, regulator, radiator hoses (top and bottom), fan belt, warning triangles, engine oil, a small coil of soft baling-wire, jump-leads, brake and clutch fluid and a full set of tools. Carry a spare set of keys and, ideally, find a place on the outside of the vehicle where they can be secured, hidden yet relatively easy to get at. Never leave the spare set in the vehicle! A tow rope and shovel are useful, so too is a hand-held spotlight.

It is only possible to give general guidelines on the availability of vehicle spares since what is required depends very much upon the make of vehicle and the particular problem. All the main centres – Gaborone, Francistown, Maun, Mahalapye, Lobatse – will stock the commonest spares for the most popular vehicles. Smaller towns, especially along the railway line, will be able to get them very quickly.

In the more remote areas garages are few and far between and proper spares almost non-existent. This is sometimes off-set, however, by the increasing levels of ingenuity and self-reliance that people in these areas have developed. In an emergency these are the people in whom your trust must be placed and, whilst you may not get a very professional job, the chances of your being able to drive on are very good.

MAPS

The main source of official maps of the country is the Department of Surveys and Lands, P/Bag 0037, Gaborone, Tel 353251. An excellent map catalogue can be obtained on request and gives detailed information as to what is available. Maps can also be purchased from the Department's offices in Selebi-Phikwe and in Francistown but stocks are limited. They carry only the large, general maps of the country and the 1 : 50 000 of their immediate areas. The offices in Maun do not sell maps although special arrangements can be made to have them collected there.

A number of commercial enterprises such as curio shops, book shops and B.G.I. sell a limited range of the more popular maps.

For those considering close and detailed work in a small area of Botswana, especially in the more remote and featureless places, aerial photographs are recommended. These 230 × 230 black and white prints are available only from the Department in Gaborone and will take a week from receipt of order. There is medium-scale cover of the entire country at 1 : 50 000, of varying ages, none more than ten years old.

Conventional six-colour maps are available in scales from 1 : 1 500 000, to the very popular 1 : 350 000 editions for the Okavango and for the Chobe areas. A mixture of monochrome and full-colour maps are available in the scales 1 : 500 000, 1 : 250 000 for the whole country, whilst a series of 1 : 100 000 and 1 : 50 000 cover the northern half, the east and the south-east of Botswana.

Street maps showing plot numbers and street names exist for Gaborone, Francistown, Selebi-Phikwe and (1987) Lobatse. A folding, pocket road map, produced on behalf of Shell Oil, can be obtained from their offices (P O Box 334, Gaborone, Telex 2437BD) and from the Department of Tourism, P/Bag 0047, Gaborone, Tel 353024.

PACKING YOUR VEHICLE

Botswana roads are rough and facilities limited. Presuming that you have planned a lengthy trip, you will have to carry a lot of equipment with you and space is at a premium.

It makes sense, therefore, to give careful thought to the way in which you pack your vehicle. Besides, cornflakes soaked in petrol don't go down very well!

There are three basic rules to follow when planning your packing:

1. Wrap hard objects with sharp edges in a cover (an old piece of underfelt or something equally substantial).
2. Pack heavy objects at the bottom of the pile.
3. Strap everything down or pack inside boxes which are strapped down.

Remember that the constant bumping and shaking, together with a copious layer of dust, will create abrasion that can rub through paint or canvas during a long journey.

You are going to be dealing with four types of gear:

1. Food and drink.
2. Camping and cooking equipment.
3. Clothing.
4. Vehicle spares and fuel.

Divide each of these into two categories: those you need immediately to hand and your bulk supplies.

Food and drink

You can get most basic foodstuffs within Botswana. It does, however, pay to plan your menus well in advance so that you have some idea of what you need to buy at what point.

It is worth carrying a large cool-box and planning for fresh meat and vegetables for the day you arrive and for 24 hours after you leave main towns. Remember, though, that Botswana is very hot, ice is not easy to come by and food will go off quickly. In addition, your vehicle's bouncing around will rapidly pulp soft vegetables and fruit, so tomatoes or peaches, for instance, don't last long. Onions and carrots do, however, and can add flavour to canned meals. Oranges are always refreshing, but don't have them in your vehicle if you are at Savuti – the elephants there have developed a taste for them.

Avoid 'pop top' plastic bottles, the type containing oil or vinegar. Pressure can pop them open at very much the wrong time. Choose screw-top containers instead.

Decant things from paper packets (eg sugar, dried milk) into screw-top containers and plan to have a '48 hour' tin that is readily to hand and a bulk supply that gets buried.

The following foodstuffs may be carried as basics:

Bannock mixture, ie flour and baking powder to make a pan bread	Oxo cubes
	Peanuts
	Raisins
Lemon juice	Rice
Instant potato powder	Butter/margarine
Stock cubes for stews etc	Muesli mix
Rusks	Bread (when available)
Glucose sweets	Cheese portions
Chewing gum	Sugar
Dried fruit	Salt
Milk powder	Pepper
Coffee	Oil
Tea bags	Vinegar

Fresh vegetables and fruit which last well include:
 Potatoes (plus tinfoil to   Carrots
  cook them in)   Oranges
 Cabbage   Lemons
 Onions

Celery and tomatoes are refreshing but don't plan to keep them too long.

The following range of tinned food is useful:
 Corned beef (an excellent base   Peas
  for stew)   Pickled fish
 Pilchards   Tomatoes
 Potatoes   Cream (for treats)
 Tomato purée (for adding   Luncheon meat
  flavour to cooked foods)   Sweetcorn
 Baked beans

All of these are good basics which can be eaten hot or cold and mixed and matched to make tasty meals. Obviously the tinned food range is enormous and you must choose according to your personal taste.

Work out your general menus in advance. You will probably find it best to pull out the food for the next 24 hours whilst in camp and pack it in a small box so that it is easy to get at. Then, if you are delayed the next day and camp late, a meal can be prepared quickly. There is nothing guaranteed to raise blood pressure more than getting into camp after dark and not being able to get a meal going until the whole vehicle has been unpacked. Everybody will probably be tired and fed up, particularly if it's raining, but a hot meal, quickly prepared, works wonders in restoring morale.

Camping gear

No experienced camper will need to be told what to carry but, for those who are a little uncertain, some guidelines are offered, drawn from personal experience.

Camping equipment in Botswana needs to fulfil a number of functions. You must be able to provide shade during the day and protection from dust and thorns on the ground. A large canvas ground-sheet is ideal for both functions. It can also be used to help vehicles out of sand, to lie under when it rains and to catch rainwater for drinking or bathing. It will also keep you warm when wrapped around your sleeping-bag.

Your camping gear must provide a totally enclosed area in which to sleep. Several incidents are recorded of lion or hyena taking a bite out of a sleeping person. It really does not make sense to sleep in the open without some kind of all-round cover, such as a lightweight tent with a built-in ground-sheet.

Camp-beds are not necessary; you can sleep on the ground. A small pillow is a good idea; unless you are practised at it, sleeping without a pillow is very uncomfortable.

Nights can be very cold during the Botswana winter when the clear open skies cause rapid heat loss from the earth. Warm sleeping gear is recommended. During the summer months mosquitoes and biting insects can be a nuisance and a tent with a fly screen or some kind of mosquito net is a good idea.

Pack your camping gear where it comes readily to hand – preferably on a roof-rack – and strap it down well before moving. Make extra sure that tent poles are firmly held in place. It is very useful to be able to get a camp set up quickly, particularly after a long day when you may have to try to do things in the dark. It is not a bad idea to practise a few times at home. It is amazing how what sounded like a simple exercise when somebody explained it to you becomes complex and nerve-racking when you try to do it in the bush, in the dark!

Cooking utensils and other basic equipment

Keep cooking equipment simple and sturdy. Glass tends to become a casualty on safari. A small gas cooker (3 kg) with a single ring is useful. Take a spare cylinder too. This is ample for three people. You can usually build a fire if you want to, but remember to collect dead wood before you arrive at campsites as the surrounding areas have usually been well stripped already.

A *potjie* (cast-iron pot), flat bottomed or three-legged, is a worthwhile investment for fire cooking. Use the following check-list for cooking equipment:

Gas cylinder plus ring	Braai grid (with clip to hold it closed)
Kettle	
Wooden platters	Plates (melamine)
Small jug (for ladling water/ soup)	Mugs
	Knives/forks/spoons
Tin-opener	Chopping knife

Thermos flask
Small spade (for toilet use, amongst others)
Plastic basin (for washing dishes, clothes and self)
Washing powder (in screw-top container)
Flat-bottomed *potjie*
Bowls
Slice
Chopping board
Small pan which can double as frying pan or cooking pan
Plastic glasses
Matches and/or lighter (waterproofed)
Paper towels
Toilet paper (in a waterproof plastic bag or container)
Two 10-litre containers of water (preferably black plastic to avoid growth of algae)
Short length of washing line and pegs
Dishwashing liquid (in screw-top container)

Divide all these things between a 'day' box and a 'kitchen' box, except the cooker and *potjie*. The 'day' box contains those things likely to be used whilst travelling – eg mugs, knives, forks, spoons, wooden platters, tin-opener. This enables you to stop and have lunch, invariably cold, without involving a major unpacking of the vehicle.

It is very useful to be able to lift the box out, collect the cooker and despatch the cook to one side to get on with the meal whilst everybody else prepares camp. This is not as easily done if the various components are scattered around all over the vehicle.

Clothing

Big suitcases tend to be a nuisance. Several canvas hold-alls are better than one large container. Because they are soft they can be packed more tightly and don't rub against other things. You can also separate your clothing into different uses with smaller containers, eg warm, night-time gear in one bag, daytime clothes in another, etc.

Plan to carry as little as is compatible with personal hygiene and comfort. You will be surprised how little you really need and clothing can be very bulky. Remember also that it is going to get crumpled up in the bags, so if you have a set of 'nice togs' for when you go out for a drink in town, they must be fairly crease-resistant.

5. CUSTOMS

BORDER POSTS

Botswana/Republic of South Africa

Border Post	Times of operation
Pont Drift	8.00 am to 4.00 pm daily
Platjan	8.00 am to 4.00 pm daily
Zanzibar	8.00 am to 4.00 pm daily
Martins Drift	8.00 am to 6.00 pm daily
Parrs Halt	8.00 am to 4.00 pm daily
Sikwane	8.00 am to 4.00 pm daily
Tlokweng Gate	7.00 am to 10.00 pm daily
Ramotswa	8.00 am to 4.00 pm daily
Pioneer Gate	7.00 am to 8.00 pm daily
Ramatlabama	7.00 am to 8.00 pm daily
Phitshane Molopo	8.00 am to 4.00 pm daily
Bray	8.00 am to 4.00 pm daily

(See also Shakawe and Ngoma Bridge below.)

Botswana/Namibia

Mamuno	7.30 am to 5.00 pm daily

Botswana/Zimbabwe

Pandamatenga	8.00 am to 4.00 pm daily (for non-commercial purposes only since there are no forwarding agents at this post)
Ramokwebana	6.00 am to 6.00 pm daily
Kazungula Road	6.00 am to 6.00 pm daily

Botswana/Zambia

Kazungula Ferry	7.00 am to 6.00 pm daily

There are a number of additional points at which Botswana can be entered where there are no border posts on the Botswana side. Entry may take place at these locations but the visitor is required to report to the nearest police station immediately. These points of entry are: Werda, Tsabong, Middlepits, Bokspits, Shakawe, Ngoma Bridge, Saambou, Baines Drift, Buffel's Drift and Pilane.

78 Botswana

Visitors should also note that there are no bridges across the Molopo River in the south, and that there are no high-level bridges across the Limpopo. Both rivers are liable to flooding and access may not then be possible.

Airports

The Sir Seretse Khama International Airport in Gaborone is open from 6.00 am to 10.00 pm through the week. Attendance outside these hours is subject to a fee payable to Customs. There are small airports at Francistown, Selebi-Phikwe, Maun and Kasane. There is no official presence at Kasane airport. The pilot is required to inform the Customs at Kazungula Road or Immigration Kasane of arrival. Passengers and their luggage must remain at the airport until clearance is effected.

Customs requirements for visitors

(a) Visitors from outside the Southern African Common Customs Area (SACCA), comprising Botswana, South Africa, Swaziland and Lesotho.

Visitors may bring into Botswana, free of duty and, where applicable, sales tax, the following:

Wine – 2 litres. Spirits and alcoholic beverages – 1 litre. Cigarettes – 400. Cigars – 50. Tobacco – 250 g. Perfume – 50 ml. Toilet water – 250 ml. Toilet soap – up to 1 kg. Other soap up to 1 kg.

Minors, i e children under the age of 18, may claim these concessions, except in respect of tobacco and alcohol.

(b) Visitors from inside the SACCA.

In general terms, there are no restrictions on what can be brought into Botswana from another country in the common customs area. There are some exceptions, however.

1. Items for which special permits are required. Permits in these cases would be obtainable from ministries concerned with Wildlife, Mines and Agriculture, among others. If you are not sure whether a permit is necessary for a particular item, enquiries should be made with the Customs authorities.
2. Items for which sales tax or duty is charged. These include beer, wines, spirits and soap. A concession is allowed for each visitor (see below). Quantities in excess of the amount allowed are subject to a duty that appears to be calculated in a number of mysterious ways

but which, we are assured, ends up, when it is charged – which is not always – by being between 10 and 20 per cent of the item's value.

Restricted items and allowances per person are as follows:

Wine – 1 litre. Beer and spirits – 1 litre. Petrol – whatever is held in the main or auxiliary tanks of the vehicle only. Toilet soap – 1 kg.

Firearms

The control of firearms in Botswana is very strict. There is a total restriction on the importation of side-arms, automatic weapons and small-bore rifles (eg of .22 calibre). An import permit is required for any permitted weapon and can be obtained by writing in advance to The Officer in Charge, Central Arms Registry, P/Bag 0012, Gaborone, Botswana.

Boats

In order to control the spread of aquatic weeds, the Department of Water Affairs requires that no boat be brought into the country without a permit. This must be applied for in advance from the Department of Water Affairs, P/Bag 0029, Gaborone (Tel 352241). Boats will not be allowed into the country without this permit.

Persons in the country moving a boat from one zone to another also require a permit which can be obtained from the same department.

Road tax

For all foreign vehicles entering the country a road tax of P5.00 is charged.

Currency

Only the following currencies are accepted by the Customs authorities: cash or traveller's cheques in rand, sterling and United States dollars; traveller's cheques only in Zimbabwe dollars.

Any amount of any currency may be imported into Botswana by any person so long as it is declared.

Any persons of any age leaving Botswana may each take out P500 in cash and the equivalent of P1 000 in cash of a foreign currency. Any amounts larger than this must be exported by means of a bank draft or by traveller's cheques. All exported cash, in any currency, must be declared at the point of exit.

Health certificates

Although the situation may change, and it is best to check with Health authorities. Inoculation certificates for TB, smallpox, yellow fever and cholera are not at the moment required.

Visa requirements

Visas are not required of passport holders from the following countries:

All Commonwealth countries, Austria, Belgium, Denmark, Federal Republic of Germany, Finland, France, Greece, Iceland, Italy, Liechtenstein, Luxemburg, Netherlands, Norway, Republic of Ireland, Republic of South Africa, San Marino, Sweden, Switzerland, United States of America, Uruguay and Yugoslavia.

Nationals of all other countries are required to obtain a visa. They should do so at least three months in advance of their intended visit, by writing to The Chief Immigration Officer, P O Box 942, Gaborone. Passport-size photographs are required for visa applications.

Pets

It is possible to bring domestic pets, such as dogs and cats, into Botswana with very little difficulty. For both dogs and cats you will need a valid rabies certificate. The rabies vaccine must have been administered not more than one year before the end of the intended journey and not less than one month before it commences. A certificate from a veterinarian, certifying that the animal is in good health, is also required.

A standard form has been drawn up by the following countries: Botswana, Lesotho, Swaziland, South Africa, Namibia and Zimbabwe. With this form, which is valid for sixty days, dogs and cats can be carried freely between each of these countries. If you bring a dog or cat with you into the country and intend that it should travel around with you, it is essential that you carry a valid permit. You will have to produce it at the numerous veterinary cordon fences through which you will pass. If you do not have such a permit, it is possible that you will not be allowed to proceed.

Visitors from Zambia, producing equivalent documents, will also be allowed to enter the country with their pets. (It should be noted, however, that dogs and cats are not allowed in National Parks or Game Reserves.)

To bring horses into Botswana, it is necessary to arrange clearance with the Veterinary Department, P/Bag 0032, Gaborone, well in advance of the intended visit. Conditions that will be imposed vary from time to time, as well as in accordance with the area from which the animal is coming. One certain requirement will be a veterinary certificate showing freedom from Dourine.

Length of stay

If a visitor wishes to remain in Botswana for a period of more than one month, he must obtain an extension of his entry permit from the nearest Immigration Department once inside the country. For non-residents, a total of ninety days a year is allowed. This regulation is strictly enforced.

MOTOR VEHICLES: LICENCES AND INSURANCE

Motor vehicles, caravans and trailers that are legitimately licensed and registered in their country of origin can be brought into Botswana by visitors and used by them for a period of 6 months. As in many other countries, all vehicles are required to hold a minimum third party insurance. Third party insurance valid in South Africa, Lesotho and Swaziland, is also valid in Botswana. Vehicles from these countries are therefore only required to pay the road tax. Vehicles registered elsewhere are required to obtain third party insurance and this can be purchased at border posts.

Foreign driver's licences are valid for 6 months. Licences not printed in English should be accompanied by a written translation.

6. DRIVING AND YOUR VEHICLE

Botswana has more than 2 500 km of first-class tarmac roads. It is now possible to drive from Johannesburg, via Gaborone and Francistown, to Kasane and through Serowe to Orapa on tar. Within a few years the tar will have reached Maun, Shakawe and Ghanzi. Increasingly excellent roads are opening up the country to the motorist.

Not all the roads, of course, are of such a good standard. There are many thousands of kilometres that range from rough or sandy tracks to gravelled surfaces and vary in quality from season to season from fair to execrable. If a good road surface is a critical factor for you, then you are advised to seek the most up-to-date information.

SPEED LIMITS

There are two speed limits in Botswana. All main roads have an upper limit of 120 km/h. In towns and villages, the general limit is 60 km/h. National parks and game reserves impose their own limits, and these are indicated in the individual reserves. The Botswana Police regularly set speed traps and offenders are prosecuted.

SAFETY BELTS

In the case of any vehicle which is fitted with safety belts, the wearing of them is compulsory. A fine of between P10 and P30 is usually imposed, although the maximum penalty is P200.

HAZARDS

The motorist is especially warned to take the very greatest care in watching for animals on the road. This is a particular hazard on roads in Botswana and many lives have been claimed in accidents caused by collision with animals. Whether a road is fenced or not, there is always the possibility of cattle, donkeys, goats and game animals straying onto the road. At night the hazard is even greater, particularly in the cooler months when animals seek the warmth of the tarmac and when, even with spotlights, dark animals on a dark road are extremely difficult to see. The danger that animals represent cannot be stressed too strongly.

We would like specially to emphasise the dangers of driving on high-speed roads at night. Many residents of Botswana regard the idea of driving on the Gaborone–Francistown road during the hours of darkness as suicidal. We suspect that when the road to Maun is tarred it will be regarded in the same way.

Despite fencing, cattle and stock will stray onto the road. Numerous people have died tragically in the last few years through collisions with animals.

Try not to drive at night on the main roads or, if you do, have very good lights and exercise the greatest caution.

ACCIDENTS

The laws in Botswana relating to the reporting of accidents are similar to those elsewhere in Southern Africa. If, as a result of a vehicle accident, there is any injury to persons or damage to property, this must be reported to the nearest police station or police officer 'as soon as is reasonably practical and in any event, within 48 hours'. Where there is minor damage only and no injury to persons, it is sufficient, with the agreement of all the parties involved, to exchange names and addresses. Where an accident has taken place it is the duty of the driver to stop. Parties involved have a legal right to demand from each other names and addresses, details of vehicle registration numbers and ownership, insurance particulars and the names and addresses of any passengers who may be potential witnesses.

A difficulty often arises in cases where livestock has been killed or injured. Basically, there are two situations in which this can happen, viz where the road is fenced and where it is not. In the former case, that is on most but not all of the tarred main roads and few, if any, of the gravel and sand roads, theoretically the owner of the animal is responsible for any death, injury or damage caused by the presence of his animals. This is because it is an offence for a stock owner to allow his animals to stray onto the road. Thus it may seem that there is a good chance of a claim against him succeeding. In practice, however, such claims are usually dismissed because of the many defences which are open to the stock owner and the counter claim of some contributory negligence on the part of the driver.

On an unfenced road it becomes even more difficult to determine responsibility for damages. In both cases therefore, being aware of the dangers, the most practical solution is to try to avoid an accident in the first place. Secondly, if you do have an accident, recognise that it is often easiest to pay compensation for the animal involved and accept the fact of damage to your vehicle. Litigation is going to be costly, lengthy and the outcome uncertain, quite apart from the fact that the owner of the animal may not have the resources to meet your damages.

VEHICLE BREAKDOWNS

Travelling in a four-wheel-drive vehicle in Botswana's remoter areas, you should be aware of the host of things that can go wrong. It is not possible, in one book, to solve all your problems but one or two hints may help in a time of crisis.

Whatever else you remember to do, there is one golden rule of critical importance. *Keep calm.* No matter how much of a hurry you are in, if you've broken down, you are going to be late. Take a break while you gain control – make a cup of tea if necessary. Above all, think about your situation before you act. Many problems are caused by very small and sometimes unlikely things coming adrift. Electrics are the most usual source of poor running or bad performance. Only as a last resort consider taking the carburettor apart!

Jacking up a vehicle

If you're stuck in mud, clay or deep sand, jack up the vehicle and put branches, planks or stones under the wheels. Sometimes, though, instead of the vehicle going up, the jack goes down, sinking into the ground! To avoid this happening, take the spare wheel off and use it as a base for the jack.

Stuck on a clay pan

Presuming that you have a winch, the problem here is that you probably have nothing to which to attach it. Take the spare wheel off and dig a trench the exact width and depth of the wheel, at right angles to the front of your vehicle and within easy reach of the winch cable. Attach the cable to the wheel and sink the wheel deeply into the trench you have dug for it. This will give you something firm to pull against.

Flat battery and unable to push-start because of sand or mud

If there is no other battery and you have a generator fitted (as opposed to an alternator), try the following. Jack up one of the driving wheels and remove it. With the car jacked up, wind a long length of cord around the hub. Ask one or two of your companions to pull on the cord, rotating the wheel. With the ignition on and the vehicle in gear, start as in a normal 'push-start' situation (foot on the clutch as the hub builds up speed; foot off the clutch when maximum speed is reached). Make sure, if you are in a forward gear, that the hub is being rotated in the right direction! If you have an alternator, this won't work.

If there is a battery handy, then use jump leads. It is usual to connect them red to red and black to black, but this only works if the 'dead' battery still has some life in it. It is much better to connect red to red and the sound battery's black to the *earth* (engine block or body-work) of the stricken vehicle, especially if it is fitted with an alternator.

If you only have one piece of lead or wire, you can make an adequate earth connection by putting the two vehicles together, metal to metal (usually bumper).

Clutch and brake fluid

You should never travel without a supply of this fluid. However, if you are caught without it, there are emergency alternatives. Almost any liquid will do – water, urine, vegetable cooking oils. *Never use mineral oils* as they will rot the rubbers. Whatever is used must be flushed out as soon as possible.

Slave or master cylinder goes

Once you are moving, you can change gears without the clutch. With a bit of practice and experience this can be done smoothly and does not harm the gearbox. The problem is getting moving in the first place. Warm the engine and then switch it off. Engage first gear, depress the accelerator and turn the starter. This is not good treatment for the starter, but it will get you going, unless you are stuck in very deep sand – in which case you have a long wait or a long walk ahead!

BUSH BEHAVIOUR

Good behaviour in the bush is like good behaviour in any circumstances. It takes the form of courtesy and consideration, an awareness of the needs of others. The major difference is that bad behaviour in the bush can be extremely dangerous or even fatal as some headlines about wildlife-human clashes in Botswana in 1984 clearly show:

"GIRL EATEN BY LION", "ELEPHANT MAULS GEOLOGY LECTURER", and "AMERICAN TOURIST BITTEN BY HIPPO".

When you see those kind of headlines you might feel that the wisest way to behave in the bush is not to go there in the first place! Not so – just be disciplined enough to follow the simple guidelines below.

There are travellers' tales aplenty about close shaves with wild animals. After all, a holiday to the wilds of Botswana is all about getting back to unspoilt Africa with its dangerous wild animals and challenges to the traveller. It may be very tempting to get so close to the elephant that its eye fills the viewfinder of your telephoto lens. Resist the temptation. It is not worth it, not only from the point of view of your own safety, but also because the more unfortunate incidents there are, the more necessary and likely it will become for the authorities to create stringent regulations and make efforts to enforce them. This will only end up curbing *your* freedom which is one of the special features of a visit to the wildlife areas of Botswana.

When driving

Keep a respectful distance from wild animals. We humans do not relish invasion of our personal space. How much less does a wild animal feel comfortable about close contact with humans and vehicles.

If you do find yourself close to animals, do some anticipatory planning and work out an escape route in case of need.

Be extremely wary of animals with young.

Do not move any distance from your vehicle unless you are accompanied by a guide who knows the area.

When camping

Never feed wild animals, although you may be tempted to do so. Resist the temptation by remembering that when you feed a wild animal you are probably signing its death warrant. One of Savuti's inhabitants was a young elephant bull. He was an affable elephant who early on discovered that one of the delights of being around tourists was that he was fed. Oranges, particularly, were an ecstatic and addictive new experience.

With his very fine sense of smell he found that he could track down oranges in tents and vehicles and he started helping himself. Sometimes helping himself required flattening a tent or breaking into a vehicle and the fact that humans were around was no deterrent.

Needless to say this behaviour brought a flood of complaints to the Department of Wildlife and National Parks and the elephant was eventually shot as a nuisance animal. Many would say that the wrong animal got the bullet.

The safari companies operating in the area ensure that they have no fruit, especially oranges, in their vehicles and our advice is to consume all your oranges and get rid of the peels before you reach Savuti.

Sleep in a tent or vehicle but never in the open. Use a tent with a built-in fly-sheet that closes firmly so that no part of your body sticks outside. An arm or a leg protruding from a tent is nothing more than effortless food.

Carry all your rubbish out of the parks. After all, you managed to carry it all in with you.

Many campers operate on the principle that empty containers take more space than full ones so they have to be thrown out. They make a great effort to ensure that no rubbish is left lying around, sometimes burying it, leaving an immaculate campsite behind. They no doubt feel very self-righteous in leaving the place in a far better condition than had their predecessors. However, it doesn't take too long before the monkeys, baboons and hyenas systematically go through the burial heap and unearth all the rubbish.

Don't camp in a hippo track. Watch out for game tracks. They appear as nice levelled areas through rough grass or bush. They vary in size and some may seem designed to let you pull your vehicle off the track and out of sight. The trouble is that they get used by their creators. If you can get a vehicle along it you've chosen an elephant, hippo or rhino track and they may come along and object – very disturbing if it happens after dark when you are asleep. So, respect other creatures' right of way and avoid problems.

This also applies to places like bridges. One party decided to sleep on the wooden bridge at Third Bridge because they had heard that the lion used it to cross the river and they were keen to see lion. They did! They also found out how difficult it was to move in a sleeping bag and to try to get six people through two Land Rover doors in a hurry. They were lucky – the lions were not hungry and did not panic and strike out.

Beware of crocodiles. When you are hot and dusty and arrive at great pools of water there is a temptation to plunge in. The Okavango has a very healthy crocodile population that includes some very large beasts. Many stretches of water will have a resident crocodile. They move very quietly and incredibly swiftly.

One unfortunate incident is recorded where a girl bathing at the edge of a pool was taken by a crocodile. The rest of the party heard a scream, ran to the water and found a cake of soap and a swirl of muddy water. The girl's body was never found.

Bathe only after you have had a thorough look around the area. Look for eyes and nostrils protruding just above the water and check along the nearby banks. Bathe with somebody keeping watch. Again the basic principle – don't be afraid but do be aware that you are in wild Africa.

BUSH DRIVING

Driving in the bush is one of those things that is 'easy when you know how'. People's responses to driving in the bush for the first time seem to be one of two extremes: either it is seen as a 'piece of cake', no different from any other driving, or they become over-anxious, as if they are about to plunge into the maw of the unknown. This over-anxiousness seems inevitably to set up a self-fulfilling prophecy and something usually does go awry.

As most of Botswana is rather like a vast beach hundreds of metres deep, your biggest challenge is likely to be sand driving. However, the tips on sand driving apply equally to mud driving. Beware the black cotton muds that occur in some areas. If it has rained, and you see an area of very black surface ahead of you, take especial care. The mud that forms in the black soils is sticky and tenacious and will thoroughly bog you down.

Be very cautious if you drive across the surface of the pans in the Makgadikgadi. The surface generally looks like a caked grey cold gravy, which may seem ideal for high speed driving. Unfortunately, under the surface it is not all the same and, without any change in appearance, you can find yourself axle-deep in cloying mud. Stay on existing tracks or, if you do move away, stay close to shore-lines.

Before you set off on your journey do make sure that you know your vehicle, especially if you are hiring or borrowing one.

The following traveller's tale is not apocryphal. It actually happened.

Next to the road was a disconsolate gaggle of hot, sweaty, dirty, anxious tourists who had been battling for well over an hour through a section of road that was really not particularly bad. They hadn't even reached the wildlife areas yet – which was probably just as well.

After the everybody-out-and-push technique had failed, they had excavated a spade from the jumble of food, camping equipment, jerry cans of water and petrol that littered the back. They had then progressed from using low technology spades to dig themselves out and were now onto high-tech winches. Neither helped much and the vehicle remained obstinately axle-deep in sand – a sobering prospect on the first day of real bush driving and in a four-wheel-drive vehicle that is supposed to be able to go just about anywhere!

It is part of the code of remote places that one always stops to lend a hand. The first Good Samaritan to arrive was fortunately bush-wise and also knew a thing or two about inexperienced drivers.

'Have you got your free-wheeling hubs engaged?' he asked. 'Our what?' they chorused.

Without going into details of the wonders of modern technology, he explained that there are gadgets on the front wheels of many four-wheel-drive vehicles that have to be switched in before you can use four-wheel-drive. Without engaging them no amount of fiddling with gears and depressing knobs will get all four wheels driving. Once engaged, it is a totally different story.

Once the free-wheeling hubs had been engaged the vehicle pulled easily out of the sand and the disconsolate group went happily on their way.

The moral of the story is, of course – make sure you know your vehicle.

Gears

The first rule is to anticipate the hazards ahead. You will soon learn to diagnose those dry sandy patches. Slow down and change into the gear in which you can negotiate the sticky patch *before* you reach it. Once you are in it, keep up your revs. If you have a rev-counter, you should not allow the engine to drop below 1 000 rpm. If this does happen, change down as quickly and smoothly as you can. Beware of 'snatching', ie accelerating too quickly, because this can shear a half-shaft or cause a wheel to spin and dig in. You need to find the balance between swiftness and smoothness.

Steering

There is a tendency to 'fight' your steering wheel, trying to make it go where you think it should. If you are in an existing track the vehicle will more or less steer itself so all you need to do is keep your hands lightly on the wheel. One of the hardest lessons to learn is that in sand a vehicle's wheels behave totally differently to anything that you will have experienced on normal roads. When it feels as though you have hauled and twisted the steering wheel so that the wheels must be pulled right around, stick your head out of the window and have a look. The chances are they are not even straight yet, never mind slewed around! It is worth the effort to find some 'tame sand' in which to practise. (Sand is 'tame' when there is someone around to help you if you get stuck!)

Tyre pressure

If you find your vehicle getting stuck in sand you can try dropping your tyre pressures. It will depend on the load you are carrying and the nature of the vehicle, but you should aim for something in the region of 1,0 kPa. This advice also applies when you are in mud. Within reason, the softer the tyre the better the traction as the tyre spreads, giving you a bigger 'footprint'. At low speeds this will not significantly shorten tyre life. Remember, however, that the likelihood of a puncture is increased and the clearance of the vehicle is lowered. This can be a problem if there is a high ridge down the middle of the track.

The Delta area is blessed (or cursed) with challenges called sand ridges, part of the old shoreline. The sand is particularly tenacious and more than one party has turned back because of the ridges. Understanding the characteristic of sand will help you to cope with this problem. As the temperature rises the tiny pockets of air between the particles of sand expand. When a heavy wheel drives over it there is a large volume of air to displace and the vehicle sinks in deep. In contrast, when it is cooler there is a smaller volume of air to displace, the sand is more compact and will support a greater weight. If you can do your sand ridge driving, therefore, in the cool of the morning, you will have fewer problems than in the heat of the day. The sand is also much more compact when wet, eg after rain.

Radiators and grass seeds

If you are driving through grass keep a close watch on your temperature gauge. As soon as the needle starts to move up, stop and check the state of the radiator. When driving through grass, or on tracks with a grassed centre, the passage of the vehicle breaks off the seed heads. These seeds then penetrate the very fine air gaps that pass through your radiator. As grass seeds accumulate they insulate the radiator, preventing the air from flowing through and the heat from dispersing. You will have to remove as much of the seed material as possible and stop until the engine has cooled down somewhat. Whatever you do, do not open the radiator when it is very hot; always let it cool down first. Modern radiators are pressurised and the sudden drop in pressure means a rapid rise in engine temperature which can damage the engine! You also run the risk of a spurt of scalding steam which can injure you.

Driving through water

Before proceeding through a patch of water, stop and examine it carefully. A walk through the water will give you some idea of its depth and the nature of the bottom. If it is even slightly risky, get into lowest range low gear, even if you don't think it necessary. It's a bit late to try to change down when you're sinking, so rather go in slowly, steadily and over-powered, than fast and under-powered. Try to avoid submerging the exhaust. A slow passage creates less turbulence and less chance of getting electrics wet.

In order to avoid excessive wetting of the engine many experts in the Delta stop and remove the fan belt when faced with a long water crossing. This action dramatically reduces the spray inside the engine compartment.

Gravel roads

Botswana has an active programme of upgrading main roads but there are still significant stretches of gravel along the main routes. If there is oncoming traffic you will find yourself enveloped in thick, blinding dust and this is *very* dangerous. There have been a number of horrific and fatal accidents on untarred main roads. These can be avoided with thought, anticipation and care. When you first see the oncoming vehicle, scan the rest of the road between you for other vehicles, pedestrians and the ubiquitous livestock. Switch on your lights so that you will be visible to any following oncoming vehicles, and slow down. Stop if you have any doubts about having a clear road ahead.

Despite the frustration of being behind a heavy truck and its billowing clouds of dust, be very cautious in trying to overtake. Rather pull over, have a cup of tea and let the vehicle ahead pull away. After all, you are on holiday and you can afford to relax rather than risk an accident.

The indigestion that results from too much, too quickly, whether it be from food, information, or visiting churches and museums, also applies to travelling. Don't be tempted into 'touring indigestion'. Plan to spend at least two nights in any one place every four days, especially if you are camping.

Driving after dark

A particular problem of driving in Botswana, as in many other remote rural areas, is livestock straying onto the road. This is especially dangerous after dark.

The situation is taken so seriously that one company forbids its employees to drive after dark, even if it means that they will be late returning to their work the following day.

Wherever possible, therefore, avoid driving after dark. If you do have to drive, then drive slowly and carefully. Good spotlights will help, but they must be well set and remember, even spotlights cannot penetrate dust and they may in fact reduce visibility through the 'bounce' of the glare on the dust.

7. FACILITIES

FACILITIES IN NATIONAL PARKS AND RESERVES

A word of caution should be sounded in introducing this section. Botswana is doing a great deal to upgrade its national parks. New facilities are being added constantly so in many of the following reserves the situation may be better than is suggested here. At the same time, although shower and toilet facilities do exist in many parks, water is frequently a problem. Supplies may be temporarily suspended for one of many reasons, including drought and the activities of game, especially elephant.

Chobe National Park

There are five public campsites – Serondela, Tjinga, Nogatsaa, Linyanti and at Savuti. All have water, toilets and showers, except Tjinga, which offers no toilet facilities.

Moremi Wildlife Reserve

Here there are four public campsites, one at either gate, each of which have showers and toilets. There is another at a place known as Third Bridge and the fourth at Xakanaxa. The latter two have toilets but no water or showers. Water may be drawn from the nearby rivers.

Nxai Pan National Park

This national park has two campsites, both with showers, toilets and water. There are also "informal" campsites at Baines' Baobabs.

Makgadikgadi and Mabuasehube Game Reserves

At Makgadikgadi a campsite has been created on the banks of the Boteti River, opposite the village of Xhumaga. Set in a large sandy area beneath beautiful, mature *Acacia erioloba*, it boasts a toilet and shower (cold water only at the moment, but hot is to come) and a stand pipe offering fresh water. Water is also available at the Game Scouts Camp.

Firewood is said to be available – but bring your own. Although a deep rubbish pit exists, we would rather take our rubbish out with us – such pits are seldom managed as they should be.

No such facilities exist at Mabuasehube, but water may be obtained at the Game Scouts Camp, although it is not wise to rely on it.

Khutse Game Reserve

There is one public campsite supplied with water and toilets.

Central Kalahari Game Reserve

Although visitors are now permitted in this reserve there are, as yet, no facilities available.

Mannyelanong Game Reserve

This reserve, created solely to protect a vulture nesting colony, has no facilities, being just a few kilometres outside the village of Otse, some 50 km south of Gaborone.

There is a nominal entry fee of P5.00 per person but road access and formal entry points are not clear and collection is somewhat haphazard.

The game reserve includes much of the mountain on which the colony is situated as well as a fenced area which demarcates the actual nesting site.

No entry whatsoever inside the fenced area is allowed. Even approaching it noisily or in haste can disturb the nesting birds and this is detrimental to their proper conservation. A handy rule of thumb? If the birds take flight as you approach, you've upset them. Be more cautious.

Kalahari Gemsbok National Park

There are three groups of lodges in this park, each with camping facilities of the highest standards. Entry to this park is through South Africa although, in unusual circumstances, it is possible to enter from Botswana. However, to do this, arrangements must be made with the Director of Wildlife and National Parks, P O Box 131, Gaborone. Tel 371405.

Gaborone Game Reserve

This new reserve, opened in 1988 on the initiative of the Kalahari Conservation Society, who deserve high praise for their great effort, is a little known gem and very well worth visiting.

Created mainly for educational purposes, it consists of 5 km^2 of varied habitat on the edge of the Ngotwane River in Gaborone. Fees, at P1,00 per person and P2,00 per car, recall the halcyon days of inexpensive game viewing!

Despite its tiny size, this remarkable reserve – when measured in terms of numbers – is the third busiest in Botswana. In 1989 more than 16 000 visitors passed through its gates!

Within the reserve will be found a wide range of mammals including white rhino, kudu, eland, wildebeest, impala, gemsbok and zebra, among others.

There is a good network of roads, a visitor's information centre and a game viewing hide. Viewing is best in the early morning and is also quite good in the evenings. The reserve opens from 6.30am to 6.30pm every day.

PARK ENTRY FEES AND REGULATIONS

National parks and game reserves in Botswana are open throughout the year. Altogether some 17 per cent of Botswana is devoted exclusively to wildlife reserves, apportioned as follows:

Three national parks: Chobe National Park, Nxai Pan National Park and the Kalahari Gemsbok National Park.

One wildlife reserve: Moremi Wildlife Reserve.

Six game reserves: Makgadikgadi Game Reserve, Central Kalahari Game Reserve, Khutse Game Reserve, Mannyelanong Game Reserve, Mabuasehube Game Reserve and Gaborone Game Reserve.

The list of fees that follows is that pertaining at the time of writing (1991).

It is possible that a review of fees may recognise the differences in the game viewing experiences offered by the different parks and reserves. It is not known if or when these changes will come about. Direct enquiries should be made at the Department of Wildlife and National Parks, tel Gaborone 371405, P O Box 131, Gaborone.

Entry Fees in Pula/day

Private parties

	Citizens	Residents	Non-residents
Over 16 years	2.00	10.00	50.00
Between 16 & 8	1.00	5.00	25.00
8 years and below	Free	Free	Free

Licenced, Botswana-based tour operators, established hotels and lodges

	Citizens	Residents	Non-residents
Over 16 years	2.00	10.00	30.00
Between 16 & 8	1.00	2.00	5.00
8 years and below	Free	Free	Free

Camping fees in Pula/night

Private parties

	Citizens	Residents	Non-residents
Over 16 years	5.00	10.00	20.00
Between 16 & 8	1.00	2.00	10.00
8 years and below	Free	Free	Free

Licenced, Botswana-based tour operators, established hotels and lodges

	Citizens	Residents	Non-residents
Over 16 years	1.00	5.00	10.00
Between 16 & 8	0.50	2.00	5.00
8 years and below	Free	Free	Free

Fishing permit in Pula/day

Citizens	Residents	Non-residents
1.00	5.00	10.00

Vehicle entrance fee in Pula/day

i)	Botswana-registered	2.00
ii)	Foreign-registered	10.00
iii)	Registered operator's vehicle (per annum)	500.00
iv)	Excess weight fee for each 450 kg over 3 500 kg unladen	250.00

Boat entrance fee in Pula/day
- i) All boats — 5.00
- ii) Operator's boats (per annum) — 150.00
- iii) Canoe/Dugout — Free

Aircraft entrance fee in Pula/day
- i) Botswana-registered — 2.00
- ii) Foreign-registered — 10.00

WHERE TO STAY IN BOTSWANA

With the growth of the tourist industry and the general development of the country there is an increasing range of places to stay in Botswana. There are still some notable gaps, however. For example, Gaborone has no caravan or camping site, and no youth hostel facilities exist anywhere.

This section is divided into three categories – Hotels, Lodges and Campsites. The hotels in the main centres of Gaborone, Francistown, Lobatse and Selebi-Phikwe are used mainly by business people and Government officials. Tourism is at present largely focused on the wildlife areas to the north, where tourist accommodation is mainly in lodges and at campsites. It is a reflection of the nature of the lodges and of tourism within the country that an important aim of this guidebook has been to try to capture something of the individual personality and ambience of these lodges.

HOTELS

Botswana in 1991 has no grading system. Price can be used as an indicator of the quality of the hotel. Many of the hotels are owned by the Botswana-based Cresta Marakanelo group and are all of a good standard.

The following is a list of the hotels and their addresses.

Francistown

Grand Hotel
Box 30
Francistown
Tel 212300. Fax 214380

Tati Hotel
Box 666
Francistown
Tel 212255

Thapama Lodge (a Cresta hotel)
P/Bag 31
Tel 213872/5
Fax 213282. Telex 2662 BD
Central reservations Tel 312431
Fax 375376. Telex 2434 BD

Marang Motel, see Lodges

Gaborone

Gaborone Sun
Private Bag 16
Tel & Fax 351111. Telex 2433 BD

Oasis Motel
P O Box 30331
Tel 356396/7. Fax 312968
Telex 2497 BD

Cresta Lodge (a Cresta Hotel)
Samora Machel Drive
P/Bag 00126
Tel 375375
Central reservations Tel 312431
Fax 375376. Telex 2434 BD

Gaborone Sheraton Hotel
P/Bag BR 105
Tel 312999. Fax 312989
Telex 2699 BD

Mogo Hotel
Box 1352
Tel 372228

President Hotel (a Cresta Hotel)
Box 200
Tel 353631. Fax 351840
Telex 2434 BD
Central reservations Tel 312431
Fax 375376. Telex 2434 BD

Morning Star Motel
Box 177
Tel 352301

Cresta Gaborone Hotel
P/Bag 00127
Tel 375200.
Fax 375201. Telex 2805 BD
Central reservations Tel 312431.
Fax 375376. Telex 2434 BD

Ghanzi

Kalahari Arms
Box 29
Tel 311

Lobatse

Cumberland Hotel (a Cresta Hotel)
Box 135
Tel 330281. Telex 2323 BD
Central reservations Tel 312431
Fax 375376. Telex 2434 BD

Lobatse Hotel
Box 800
Tel 330157

Mahalapye
    Mahalapye Hotel
    Box 526
    Tel 410200

Maun, see Lodges

Molepolole
    Mafenya-Tlala
    P/Bag 10
    Tel 320394

Palapye
    Palapye Hotel (a Cresta Hotel)
    Box 1
    Tel 420277

    Botsalo Hotel (a Cresta Hotel)
    Box 35
    Tel 420245
    Fax 420587. Telex 2698 BD
    Central reservations Tel 312431
    Fax 375376. Telex 2434 BD

→Selebi-Phikwe
    Bosele (a Cresta Hotel)
    Box 177
    Tel 810675/6/7
    Fax 811083. Telex 2201 BD
    Central reservations Tel 312431
    Fax 375376. Telex 2434 BD

    Syringa Lodge
    PO Box 254
    Tel 810444. Fax 810450

Serowe
    Serowe Hotel
    Box 150
    Tel 430234

    Tshwaragano
    Box 102
    Tel 430377

Tuli Block
    Zanzibar Resort and Lodge
    (reopened January 1991)
    PO Box 20523
    Gaborone
    Tel 356396 (c/o Oasis Motel)
    Fax 352511

100 Botswana

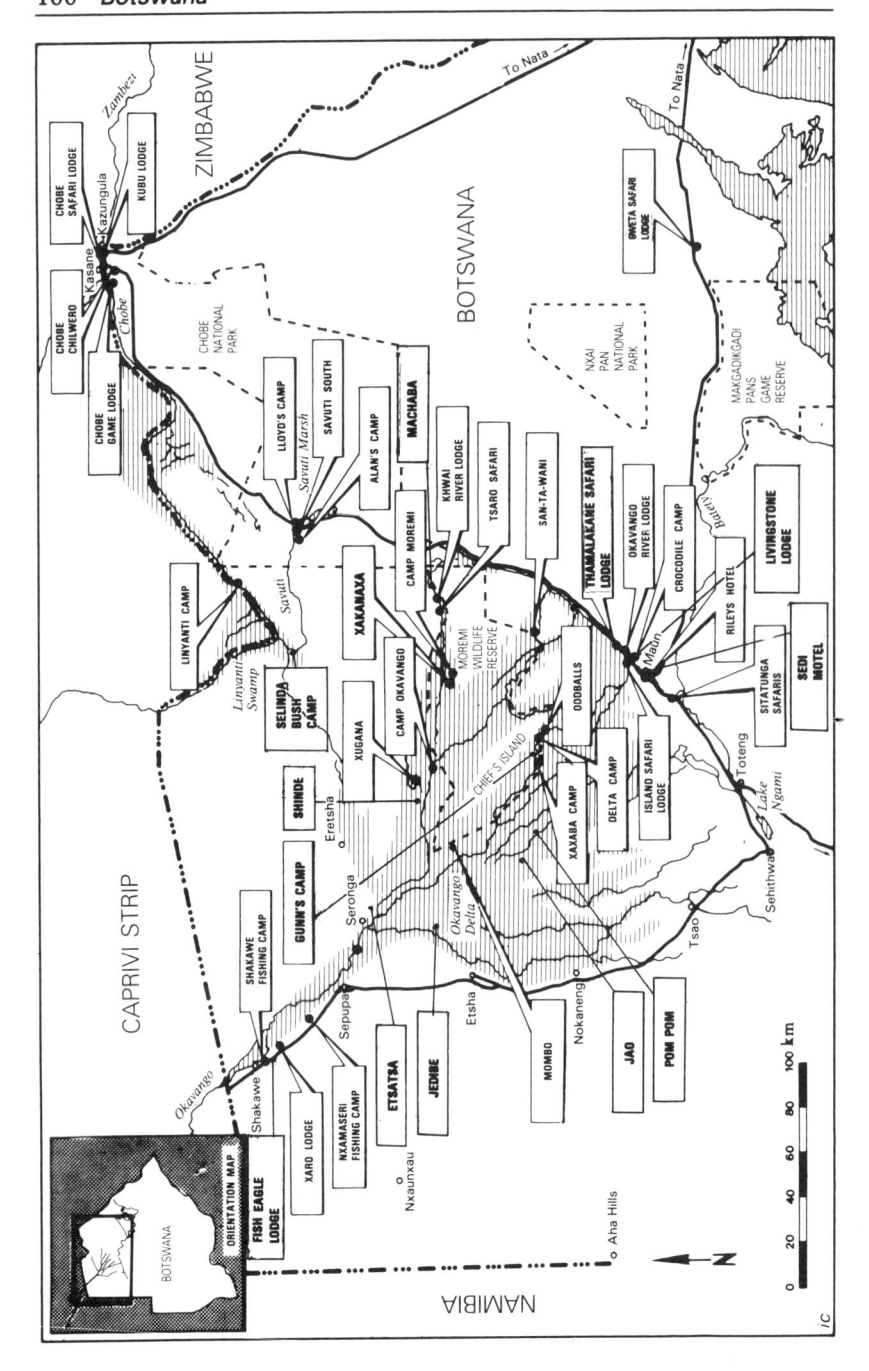

LODGES

The tourist industry of Botswana is comparatively young. The first lodge was a hunting lodge built in the late sixties. Staying in a lodge is not the same as staying in a five-star emporium, and a lodge will not offer the predictable sameness of hotel chains that you might find anywhere else in the world. Each lodge has its own character and this is especially true of those which are individually owned. You may well enjoy five-star service but it will be very different from that which is laid down in the list of requirements for a grading system.

As you read through the descriptions of the lodges in this section you should be able to develop a feel for what to expect. This section is intended to help you choose where to stay and how to construct the kind of Botswana holiday experience that will suit both your interests and your pocket.

The lodges are grouped by area and the areas are arranged in alphabetical order. At the beginning of each section there is a brief description of the area.

Heading each lodge description is a summary; this is for quick reference to determine the type of accommodation offered, the tariff level, facilities and activities.

List of Lodges in Botswana (by area)

FRANCISTOWN	The Marang
GWETA	Gweta Safari Lodge
KASANE	Chobe Chilwero
	Chobe Game Lodge
	Chobe Safari Lodge
	Kubu Lodge
MAUN	Crocodile Camp Safaris
	Island Safari Lodge
	Livingstone Lodge
	Okavango River Lodge
	Riley's Hotel
	Sedi Motel
	Sitatunga Safaris
	Thamalakane Safari Lodge

MOREMI & CENTRAL DELTA	Camp Moremi Camp Okavango Camp Okuti Delta Camp Gunn's Camp Jao Khwai River Lodge Machaba Oddballs Pom Pom San-ta-wani Shinde Tsaro Safari Xakanaxa Xaxaba Camp Xugana
SAVUTI	Alan's Camp Linyanti Lloyd's Camp Savuti South Selinda Bush Camp
NATA	Nata Lodge
TULI	Jwala Game Lodge Mashatu Game Reserve Stevensford Game Reserve Tswana Safaris Tuli Lodge
WESTERN DELTA	Etsatsa Fish Eagle Lodge Jedibe Nxamaseri Fishing Camp Shakawe Fishing Camp Xaro Lodge

Francistown area

This is not usually a major port of call for tourists. It is one of the older towns in the country and is the hub of economic activity in the area. It has good road and rail links to major sources of supply so, from the visitor's point of view, it is a good place to pick up motor spares and basic necessities.

THE MARANG Tariff: Budget (camping) Medium (hotel)
PO Box 807, Francistown, Tel 213991/2/3. Fax 12130. Telex 2264 BD.

Accommodation	Facilities	Activities/ Attractions
Hotel with rooms	Licensed	Birdlife
Rondavels and chalets	Restaurant	Walks
Camping	Swimming pool	Golf
Booking advisable	Telephone	
	Telex	
	Conference room	
	Packed lunches	
	Tourist advice and maps	
	Satellite TV	

Just outside Francistown, on the banks of the Tati River, you will find the Marang, 'the place of sunbeams'. Huge acacia trees, lush green lawns, thatched roofs and genuine comfort all make the Marang an outstanding hotel.

Choose from wood and thatch chalets by the river bank, or air-conditioned rooms or rondavels. Whichever you decide on, you will enjoy the beauty and tranquillity this hotel offers.

The atmosphere is relaxed and friendly and in these surroundings, like many guests before you, you will leave intending to return again.

The Marang also has a beautiful, shady campsite with hot water and clean ablution blocks. There is a terrace and an excellent à la carte restaurant, a swimming pool, conference room and a most attractive bar constructed out of kiaat wood from Nata.

The Marang has become 'the place' to stop over on the long road to the Okavango and Chobe – don't miss it!

Gweta area

A small village, just off the main tourist route, becomes an attraction because of the Gweta Safari Lodge.

GWETA SAFARI LODGE Tariff: Budget
P O Box 124, Gweta. Also Maun,Tel 612220. Fax 660493. Telex 2487 BD.

Accommodation	Facilities	Activities/ Attractions
Motel Camping	Licensed Restaurant Shop Curios Take-away food Swimming pool Fuel	Birdlife Game viewing Game drives

Gweta lies just off the gravel main road from Francistown to Maun, some 99 km west of Nata. The rest camp is well signposted and is worth the detour.

Gweta, an appealing village, as yet not too tarnished with the brick and corrugated-iron blight of so many rural villages, is set among tall palm trees. Gweta Safari Lodge – gateway to the Makgadikgadi Pans and game reserve – is very much a part of the local community and for travellers wishing to meet the people of the country, the pleasant bar, with its well-used dart-board, is the place to go.

There is a restaurant with a respectable à la carte menu; lighter meals are served under the thatched umbrellas outside. A take-away menu is also offered. Accommodation consists of brick cottages under thatch and tariff includes dinner, bed and breakfast, or bed and breakfast, or just bed. An attractive, serviced camping ground is nearby.

A delightful selection of African curios is available at the motel reception. There is a shop that stocks everything a rural villager could want, a bottle-store and a fully equipped vehicle workshop where minor repairs and welding can be undertaken.

Game drives into the Makgadikgadi Pans and game reserve can be organised, and there are plans for horse trails to be developed. Both of these involve that redoubtable Makgadikgadi character, Jack Bousfield. The former is underway and there can be few more exotic, exciting and original ways to see the magnificent Makgadikgadi than from the seat of the special 'All Terrain Vehicles' (ATVs) that Jack uses.

To find out more about these remarkable safaris, ask Margie at Gweta to help you arrange one or make direct contact with Kalahari-Kavango Safaris. (See list of Mobile Operators on page 147 of this guide.)

Kasane area

Kasane is currently experiencing considerable growth and the consequent development of its infrastructure. Tourism is certainly one of the driving forces, and the completion of the tar road from Nata has made the area very much more accessible.

There is an ever-growing range of food and liquor available here. You can buy diesel and petrol and some repairs can be undertaken at Chobe Engineering, which is a few kilometres out of town on the Kazungula road.

CHOBE CHILWERO Tariff: High
P O Box 22, Kasane. Tel Kasane 250234. Telex 2763 BD.

Accommodation	Facilities	Activities/Attractions
Chalets Booking essential	Licensed Gift shop Radio	Birdlife Game viewing Cruises Game drives Game flights Boating

Chobe Chilwero is perched on top of the small escarpment between Kasane and the main entrance to the Chobe National Park. Take the road out of Kasane to the National Park. Just past Chobe Safari Lodge, look for a road to the left that crosses a small culvert bridge and heads up the hill. Follow this road for 5 km. Kasane is also accessible by air and guests can arrange to be collected from the airstrip.

Chilwero is a beautiful example of imaginative building, using local materials. Poles and thatch have been used boldly in the double-storey main building, which nestles under a magnificent sweep of thatched roof. The dining-room is dominated by a vast refectory table, made locally of kiaat, an indigenous tree famed for the splendour of its wood.

Around the striking central building are eight individual chalets with en suite shower, basin and toilet. Sited 100 m above the plain below, Chilwero offers some of the best views in Botswana.

Chilwero is run by Brian and Jan Graham and one is assured, within this exclusive retreat, of their personal attention. Rates include accommodation, game viewing, meals, and laundry, but they do not cover liquor. Game drives are carried out by professional guides.

CHOBE GAME LODGE Tariff: High
P O Box 32, Kasane. Tel 250340. Telex 2765 BD. Also P O Box 2602, Halfway House, 1685, South Africa. Tel (011) 3151695. Fax (011) 805 2882. Telex 421083 SA.

Accommodation	*Facilities*	*Activities/ Attractions*
Hotel	First aid	Birdlife
Booking essential	Licensed	Game viewing
	Restaurant	River cruises
	Swimming pool	Game drives
	Shop	Fishing
	Telephone	Game flights
	Radio	Boating
	Fuel	

Chobe Game Lodge is 12 km west of Kasane. Drive through the town towards the Chobe National Park. The road changes to a firm, but frequently corrugated dirt road. Four kilometres outside Kasane is the entrance to the National Park. You will have to stop at the gate, fill in the appropriate forms and pay the park entrance fees. Visitors arriving at the gate and producing proof of their reservations will be charged the lower 'Operators' park fees. There is a main road that leads directly to the Game Lodge, or you can choose various scenic options.

Chobe is a place of contrasts. In the midst of the African bush it is an enclave of luxury. Green lawns and lush gardens contrast with dry, dusty, wintry landscapes.

From the spacious entrance hall, a gallery of striking African art, the main building steps down to a river vista. It is a place of romance and has worked its magic on many people, perhaps the best known being Liz Taylor and Richard Burton, who celebrated their second marriage here in 1976.

Accommodation is in pleasingly appointed rooms with bathrooms en suite. For those who desire privacy, and can afford its price, there is a luxury suite with its own private swimming pool. Other guests have access to the large communal pool set in lawns on the river bank. The hotel is currently planning a discount system in its accommodation rates for all bona fide citizens and residents of Botswana. Members of the Kalahari Conservation Society will receive, on production of a valid membership card, a 25 per cent discount on the Botswana bed and breakfast rate.

Amidst this luxury, it is all too easy to forget that you are a guest in the domain of the animals. Be prepared for reminders such as bushbuck grazing on the lawns, the colourful birdlife, troops of baboons and even elephants and hippos, which come to feed on the trees and green lawns.

If the lure of big game has brought you to Chobe, you can go game-viewing by boat or by open motor vehicle, if you do not have your own. Early morning and late afternoon are the best times for this. The hotel has a Cessna 207 at Kasane airstrip and can provide flights to Moremi, Savuti, Okavango or Victoria Falls. For the rest, there is the appeal of relaxing beside the pool, or taking a 'booze-cruise' which combines game viewing by boat, watching the sunset and ice-cold refreshment after the heat of the day.

CHOBE SAFARI LODGE Tariff: Medium
P O Box 10, Kasane, Tel 250336. Telex 2762 BD.

Accommodation	*Facilities*	*Activities/ Attractions*
Hotel	First aid	Birdlife
Chalets	Licensed	Game viewing
Camping	Restaurant	River cruises
Booking essential	Swimming pool	Fishing
	Shop	Game drives
	Telephone	Game flights
	Fuel	Boating
	Cocktail lounge	Canoes

Chobe Safari Lodge is on the western outskirts of Kasane, overlooking the Chobe River. Once you have reached Kasane, take the main road towards the National Park and you will see the hotel on the right-hand side of the road, just before you leave town.

Apart from the hotel itself, there are chalets and camping facilities. This is a popular spot for fishermen and you can hire boats to take you further afield than just the river banks. Game drives can be arranged and, when you are neither game viewing nor fishing, you can cool off in the residents' pool. A daily river cruise, on a twenty-five seater, double-decker boat, is arranged by the hotel. The vessel has bar facilities and is excellent for bird and game viewing.

The hotel is conveniently located close to a bank, garage, general store and liquor store.

KUBU LODGE Tariff: Medium
P O Box 43, Kasane. Tel 250312. Fax 250223. Telex 2768 BD.

Accommodation	Facilities	Activities/Attractions
Hotel	Licensed	Birdlife
Chalets	Restaurant	Game viewing
Camping	Swimming pool	Walks
Booking essential	Tennis courts	Game drives
	Shop	Fishing
	Telephone	Boating
		Mobile Safaris

Take the tar road from Kasane to Kazungula. Some 10 km from Kasane you will see signs to Kubu Lodge that will direct you down towards the river. The Lodge is about 1 km from the main road.

Kubu Lodge used to be the site of The Employment Bureau of Africa (TEBA) recruitment office for the Kasane area. It bears many signs of the old colonial era, with exotic trees, such as jacarandas and flamboyants, planted round the settlement. The old houses have wide verandas which are closed in with mosquito gauze.

Among large and ancient trees are eleven wooden chalets with thatched roofs, overlooking the Chobe River and offering comfortable accommodation. There is a two-storey restaurant of wood and thatch with a small cocktail bar, a lounge and an extensive balcony with a superb and refreshing view. This is the place for a sundowner in every sense of the word! The kitchen produces excellent home-cooked meals.

The swimming pool is a delight in the heat of a Kasane summer and is a welcome facility even in the middle of winter. For the energetic, there is a tennis court and, for further recreation, boats can be hired and used on the river. In addition, there are daily game drives in open Land Rovers with professional guides to Chobe National Park.

Campsites are laid out along the river and there are brick and thatch ablution facilities of a high standard. As part of maintaining the 'quality' of camping life, numbers are restricted and so it is advisable to book during the busy seasons of Easter, June and July.

It is from Kubu Lodge that Denis Van Eyssen, under the name GO WILD, arranges tailor-made vehicle safaris, either on a local scale in the Chobe area or, if you like, further afield into the Okavango, Nxai Pan or Makgadikgadi. He can be contacted through Kubu Lodge.

Maun area

Maun is the main administrative town for the north-western districts and many Government offices are situated here. The main tourist areas are clustered around the tarred roads of the town.

In Maun you can buy most of the basics that you might need to keep yourself and your vehicle in reasonable shape. The combination of goods available is a pithy comment on the type of shoppers found in Maun. It is possible to buy a sola topi with a battery-powered fan set into the brim and, with equal ease, a cast-iron, three-legged cooking pot.

Maun has a large population of Hereros, refugees from Namibia at the turn of the century. The strikingly dressed women in their long, colourful, Victorian dresses will tempt the photographer to whip out his camera. Be warned, though, for unless you have previously negotiated both the photograph and the payment, you will not be popular.

After some years of controversy, there seems little doubt that the much discussed 'Lake Maun' will finally go ahead. It is rumoured, at the time of writing, that construction has already started.

Damming of the Boteti and Thamalakane will create a large reservoir whose primary aim will be to ensure a steady supply of water for Maun and for Orapa Diamond Mine (via the Boteti).

The reservoir itself will have a dramatic effect on Maun. The maximum water level will be about a metre below the underside of the Francistown Bridge.

The presence of such a large body of water may see the introduction of aquatic sports and activities on a wide scale. We can expect to see the emergence of power boating, canoeing, river cruises and the like. Maun may never be the same again and the operations of all the riverside hotels, camps and lodges will inevitably be extended.

CROCODILE CAMP SAFARIS Tariff: Medium
P O Box 46, Maun. Tel 660265. Fax 660493. Telex 2487 BD.

Accommodation	Facilities	Activities/Attractions
Chalets	Licensed	Birdlife
Camping	Restaurant	Mekoro
Booking essential	Telephone	Game drives
	Radio	Fishing
		Boating
		Canoes

'Croc Camp' must be one of the best known camps in Botswana. Started by the famous crocodile hunter, Bobby Wilmot, it is one of the oldest tourist camps in the Maun area. It is situated on the bank of the Thamalakane River, the water level of which varies according to the time of year and the nature of the annual floods.

Access to this camp has improved since the road to Sherobe has been tarred. Leave Maun on the Nata road and turn left (north) after crossing the bridge over the Thamalakane. Crocodile Camp is about 12 km away on the road to Moremi.

Close to the river are reed and thatch cottages with self-contained showers and flush toilets. Also set amongst the riverside trees is the focal point of the camp – the bar. There is an excellent restaurant and 'Croc Camp' proudly claims the best food in Maun!

The camping area is set back from the river. Individual sites are separated by reed fences and there is an ablution block with hot and cold showers and flush toilets.

Crocodile Camp Safaris, as their name suggests, also organise a wide range of mobile safaris, both by boat and vehicle, into the Okavango and throughout Botswana. Each safari is accompanied by a licensed professional guide. For more details the owner Karl-Heinz Gimpel or Jane Elliot should be contacted.

ISLAND SAFARI LODGE Tariff: Medium
P O Box 116, Maun, Tel 660300. Fax 660205. Telex 2482 BD.

Accommodation	*Facilities*	*Activities/ Attractions*
Hotel	First aid	Birdlife
Chalets	Licensed	Game viewing
Camping	Restaurant	Walks
Booking advisable	Swimming pool	River cruises
	Shop	Game drives
	Telephone	Fishing
	Game park	Game flights
		Boating
		Canoes
		4 × 4 Vehicle hire

Starting from Maun, take the tar road north-west from the junction near the airport. Continue on when the tar stops. After a total of some 10 km, just before the Matlhapaneng bridge, you will see, on your left-hand side, signposts directing you towards Island Safari Lodge.

The lodge is situated under a canopy of fine old trees and one is aware of constant birdsong and the chatter of squirrels. The two-, three- or four-bedded brick cottages are thatched and all have hot and cold showers. There is a restaurant and bar and films are shown twice weekly.

The campsite is also set among the trees lining the river and there are good ablution facilities. The birdlife is a constant delight, even if you are not a keen birdwatcher.

LIVINGSTONE LODGE Tariff: Medium
P/Bag 10, Francistown. Tel 611210. Fax 611210.

This new lodge will be built during 1991. It will offer accommodation in luxury furnished safari tents on a site 14 km outside Maun (on the tarred Sherobe/Moremi road) right on the banks of the Thamalakane River and close to Crocodile Camp, Island Safari and Okavango River Lodge.

There will be a restaurant, bar and swimming pool and ablution facilities in reed and thatched enclosures which will also be available for campers.

In time, the lodge intends to offer canoe and mekoro excursions as well as safaris into the Okavango Delta. Boat hire, sundown cruises, walking trails, air charter and mobile safaris through Botswana will also be on its bill of fare.

OKAVANGO RIVER LODGE Tariff: Medium
P O Box 32, Maun. Tel 660298. Telex 2482 BD.

Accommodation	Facilities	Activities/Attractions
Chalets	First aid	Birdlife
Camping	Licensed	Mekoro
Booking advisable	Restaurant	River cruises
	Swimming pool	Fishing
	Shop	Boating
	Telephone	Canoes
	Pool bar	Paddle-boats
	Bottle-store	

Okavango River Lodge is located approximately 11 km north-east of Maun on the Moremi road. It can be approached from either side of the river.

In the heat of Botswana a swimming pool is a great drawcard and this lodge's pleasant pool is no exception. To immerse oneself in cool water without the company of hippo, crocs and other water beasties is a welcome attraction.

You can stay in the two-, three- or four-bedded brick cottages, each with hot and cold showers. Alternatively, one can camp alongside the river, where showers and flush toilets are provided.

RILEY'S HOTEL (a Cresta Hotel) Tariff: High

P O Box 1, Maun. Tel 660204, 660320. Fax 660580. Telex 2418 BD. Central Reservations Tel 312431. Fax 375376. Telex 2434 BD.

Accommodation	Facilities	Activities/ Attractions
Hotel Booking essential	Licensed Restaurant Shop Telephone Radio Off-sales	See below

Riley's Hotel is in the centre of Maun, on the river side of the tar road (see map). The original hotel, with its unique frontier atmosphere, has been substantially renovated. Ever expanding to meet the energetic growth of Maun, Riley's now has 50 double air-conditioned rooms with bathrooms, as well as three suites. The large and immaculate swimming pool is extremely popular, as are Harry's Bar and the Motswiri Pool bar.

Deep, shady verandas surround two sides of the hotel and look down onto the river. It is a splendid observation post for the keen photographer, who might even catch a hippo passing surreptitiously by.

Riley's is within easy walking distance of banks, curio shops, a garage, and fresh produce and liquor stores.

SEDIE MOTEL Tariff: Medium

P O Box 29, Maun. Tel 660297.

This motel-to-be is another product of the burgeoning tourist industry in Maun. At the time of writing it was due to open by June 1991.

It is located 5 km from Maun on the road to Matlapaneng and is on the south-west side of the Thamalakane. Take the tar road out of town north-west from the airport junction.

The motel has 24 double rooms and a restaurant. There are also 6 cottages, each with a double bed and two single beds for those who wish to self-cater. All are relatively near the river. In time there will be a swimming pool and tennis court.

SITATUNGA CAMPING SAFARIS Tariff: Budget

P/Bag 47, Maun. Tel & Fax 660570. Telex 2618 BD.

Accommodation	*Facilities*	*Activities/ Attractions*
Camping	First aid	Birdlife
Booking advisable	Licensed	Walks
Chalets	Shop	Fishing
	Radio call	Crocodile Farm

Approaching Maun from the direction of Nata, cross the Thamalakane River and turn left, on the tar road, at the T-junction in front of you. The camp is a further 12 km, on the left, and is well marked with signs to the crocodile farm.

The general camping area is situated at the main entrance to Sitatunga Camp and is attractively laid out in a well-wooded area. Taps bring water to the campsites and firewood is provided. There are hot showers and flush toilets. An unique attraction of this camp site (which does not provide meals, by the way) is John Seaman's Crocodile Farm with which it shares the property and which you are invited to tour by arrangement with the staff. A shop sells general provisions and liquor at the entrance to the campsite.

THAMALAKANE SAFARI LODGE Tariff: Medium
P/Bag 22, Maun. Tel 660307. Fax 660307. Telex 2613 BD.

Accommodation	Facilities	Activities/ Attractions
Chalets	First aid	Birdlife
Booking not essential	Restaurant	Mekoro
	Licensed	Boating
	Swimming pool	Game drives

The lodge is some distance north of Maun on the road to Moremi. Approximately 15 km out you will come to a fork in the road. Take the left fork and continue for a further 5 km. The camp is signposted. The sand on this road can be bad and a four-wheel-drive vehicle is preferable.

Thamalakane Safari Lodge is a pleasant stopover from the heat and dust of travelling in Ngamiland. It is located on the bank of the Thamalakane River and the site makes the best use of the available trees.

There are brick under thatch chalets, each with a wash-basin and some with showers. Outside ablution facilities are good.

Apart from enjoying walks, the birdlife and the tranquillity of the river-front, Thamalakane Lodge organises some exciting and worthwhile safaris into the Delta, using vehicles and boats. These trips can be tailored to your personal requirements.

Moremi area

Moremi is probably the Mecca of the wildlife enthusiast. There are no places to buy food or fuel in this area so once you leave Kasane or Maun to enter Moremi you must be fully self-contained. A four-wheel-drive vehicle is essential. The country is flat and well vegetated, with extensive areas under water after the annual flooding. There are four camping areas in Moremi – at North and South gates, Third Bridge and Xakanaxa.

CAMP OKAVANGO Tariff: High
P/Bag 10, Maun. Tel 660564/9. Telex 2617 BD.

Accommodation	Facilities	Activities/ Attractions
Tented camp	Licensed	Birdlife
Booking essential	Restaurant	Game viewing
	Radio	Walks
		River cruises
		Fishing
		Flights
		Boating

Camp Okavango is not open to the casual visitor. It is essential to book in advance and you will then be flown into the camp or taken by boat from the sister Camp Moremi.

This is truly a taste of gracious living in the bush. Everywhere are the thoughtful touches of Jessie Neil who created the camp, celebrating her love affair with this special part of the wild world. Expect the unexpected. The bar's splendid array of liquor made everywhere else in the world, a silver tea service and silver candelabra, bats roosting over the elegantly set tea table, the strange, evocatively mournful call of the hippo drum calling guests to meals.

Keep your eyes open for the quietly unobtrusive grace notes – the bird-bath inscribed 'For all you beautiful gifts of God', the glory boxes in your tent, bathroom and on the boat which carry everything you might conceivably need to make your visit comfortable.

Accommodation is in spacious tents with reed ablution blocks close by. When you are not eating or drinking the seemingly never-ending fare, you will be taken out game-viewing, bird-watching or fishing. Your only transport through the surrounding waterways is by boat. You may also ask to be taken to islands to walk the wild.

CAMP MOREMI Tariff: High
P/Bag 10, Maun. Tel 660564/9. Telex 2617 BD.

Accommodation	*Facilities*	*Activities/ Attractions*
Tented camp	Licensed	Birdlife
Booking essential	Restaurant	Game viewing
	Radio	Game drives
		Flights

Although Camp Moremi is accessible by road to the independent traveller, casual visitors are definitely not welcome. The camp is situated on the Xakanaxa lagoon in the heart of the Moremi Reserve.

Camp Moremi is the younger sister of Camp Okavango and is a bolder, more extravagant celebration of Jessie Neil's love of the area. So much of the surrounding terrain is flat that to create a special vista one has to float above ground and this is just what has been done as the lounge and dining area have been built up on tall stilts among the trees that line the banks of the lagoon, giving a magnificent 'tree tops' feel.

Accommodation is in a luxurious tented camp with adjacent reed and thatch ablution facilities.

CAMP OKUTI Tariff: Medium
P/Bag 49, Maun. Tel & Fax 660307. Telex 2618 BD.

Accommodation	Facilities	Activities/Attractions
Chalets	Licensed	Birdlife
Booking essential	Restaurant	Game viewing
	Bar	Boating
	Radio	Game drives
		Mekoro
		Canoes
		Walks
		Fishing

Camp Okuti is situated in the Moremi Reserve on the banks of the Xakanaxa Lagoon. It is accessible by road or by air from Maun.

The camp is privately owned by Rolf and Helma Schleipfer and has a delightful informal atmosphere. To help preserve this asset the number of guests is limited to a maximum of 14 persons.

The accommodation is enchanting, with comfortable A-frame thatched chalets sheltering beneath tall trees and overlooking the beautiful lagoon. The daily rate includes all activities, all meals and all drinks.

A visit to Camp Okuti is a special experience for those who like to combine in one safari the attractions of both the Okavango Delta and the rich and exciting game viewing opportunities of the Moremi Game Reserve.

DELTA CAMP Tariff: High
P O Box 39, Maun. Tel 660220. Fax 660589. Telex 2484 BD.
Also Box 52900, Saxonwold, 2132, South Africa. Tel (011) 788 5549. Fax 788 6575. Telex 422302 SA.

Accommodation	Facilities	Activities/Attractions
Chalet	Licensed	Birdlife
Booking essential	Radio	Game viewing
		Mekoro
		Walks
		Fishing

There is no access to this camp by road, so it is not a place for a casual visit. Arrangements to fly in must be made. There are daily flights to the camp from Maun.

Delta is one of the oldest camps in the Okavango. It nestles unobtrusively under tall trees, the reed, wood and grass of which it is built blending harmoniously with the setting. The activities of Delta focus on bird-watching, game viewing and fishing. It is a good place from which to explore the waters of the Okavango by mokoro.

All meals, drinks and excursions are included in the daily tariff.

GUNN'S CAMP Tariff: Budget
P/Bag 33, Maun. Tel 660351. Fax 660571. Telex 2612 BD.

Accommodation	*Facilities*	*Activities/ Attractions*
Camping	Licensed bar	Mekoro
Bungalows	Meals	Boat safaris
	Shop	Game viewing
	Radio	Game walks
		Birdlife
		Fishing
		Flights

There is no way into Mike Gunn's camp unless you fly or go by boat. On the Boro River, opposite Chief's Island in the Moremi Reserve, the camp is set on two small, neighbouring islands, each densely wooded and graced with tall palms.

On one island is the camping site with its toilets and showers available to campers. The second island offers comfortable, serviced, four-bedded bungalows each with its own toilet and shower, linen, mosquito nets, etc.

Groups occupying a bungalow may cater for themselves and will find their accommodation equipped with basic crockery, cutlery and a gas stove. If guests do not select this option, all meals are available, by arrangement, and at extra cost.

Mokoro safaris can be arranged while in the camp. People may go out for two or three days or, sometimes, just for a few hours. To avoid overcrowding and spoiling this priceless atmosphere no more than twenty mekoro are authorised to operate from these islands.

Two factors make Gunn's camp unique. By arrangement with the owners, trans-Okavango boat safaris can be organised and Mike Gunn also runs 'made-to-order' fitness and wilderness courses.

JAO Tariff: Medium
P O Box 119, Maun. Tel 660383 or 660571. Fax 660593.
Also P O Box 651171, Benmore, 2010, South Africa. Tel (011) 884 1458/9. Fax 883 6255. Telex 428642 SA.

Accommodation	Facilities	Activities/Attractions
Luxury tents	Licensed	Game drives
Booking essential	Restaurant	Game walks
	Radio	Mekoro
	First Aid	Fishing
	Airstrip	

Jao is considered by many to be one of the loveliest camps in the Okavango. One of the most westerly, it is far from the large river systems yet is still in the permanent part of the Delta facing on to its own delightful (and private) lagoon.

The camp is on a small island which is reached from the 'mainland' by means of a quaint wooden bridge. It is set among towering evergreens that keep the warmth in winter and the place cool and shady during the hot summers.

Jao is normally reached by air, clients being met by vehicle and driven a short distance to the island, although the camp does have a (long) road link with Maun and can also be reached by boat.

Located on the western edge of the !Xo flats, there are remarkable opportunities for walking among the game on innumerable islands. You can also travel by mekoro and slide silently through the reeded river channels to encounter the prolific birdlife at close quarters. We are told that the fishing is outstanding.

KHWAI RIVER LODGE Tariff: Medium
P O Box 100, Maun. Tel 660302. Telex 2648 BD *or*
Gametrackers, c/o Safariplan, P O Box 4245, Randburg, 2192, South Africa. Tel (011) 886 1810. Fax 886 1815.

Accommodation	Facilities	Activities/Attractions
Hotel	First aid	Birdlife
Booking essential – only through Gametrackers Safari Programmes	Licensed	Game viewing
	Swimming pool	Walks
	Shop	Game drives
	Radio	Canoeing (seasonal)

Khwai is not a casual, drop-in destination – so make prior arrangements if you intend to spend a night or have a meal there. From the north gate of the Moremi Reserve, head in an easterly direction for 8 km. There are a number of roads to choose from, so direction finding is something of an act of faith. The lodge overlooks the river.

Khwai Lodge, part of the Gametrackers organisation, is one of the largest lodges in the Delta. The thatched main complex of dining-room, bar and lounge is open to the elements. After your evening meal, coffee, liqueurs and tales of the day are served up around the fire outside. Accommodation is in separate, individual chalets scattered among the trees. Each has its own shower, basin and toilet.

Game drives take clients into the reserves to see the wildlife. The rest of the time can be spent around the pool, or viewing the birds and game from the grounds of the lodge. Keep a beady eye for elephants which love the lodge's young fig trees. The elephants are no respecters of humans who might be in their way.

Khwai's resident hippo are a source of great interest. It is hard to believe that these creatures, which look so somnolent in the water, are the animals apparently responsible for the greatest number of human deaths in Africa.

MACHABA Tariff: Medium

Kerr Downey & Selby, P O Box 40, Maun. Tel 660211-3. Fax 660379. Telex 2485 BD.

Accommodation	*Facilities*	*Activities/ Attractions*
Luxury tents	Licensed	Game drives
Booking essential	Restaurant	Night drives
	Radio	Birdlife
	First Aid	

Machaba lies in the heart of big game country on the banks of the Khwai River with Moremi Game Reserve right opposite.

You can drive in but most people fly and there is a short transfer from the airstrip to the camp.

Accommodation is in luxury tents with every convenience thought of and really good showers and ablutions. Few things recapture the magic of the passing Africa like the long evenings of conversation and convivial company round a blazing campfire in the middle of a tented camp.

For the photographer, apart from the remarkable birdlife, there is an enormous range of game animals to choose from, both in the reserve and outside it. Leopard, elephant, buffalo, lion and giraffe can all be expected. The night game drives are a fascinating experience and open another dimension of the wilderness experience.

ODDBALLS Tariff: Budget–Medium
P O Box 39, Maun. Tel 660220. Fax 660589. Telex 2484 BD.
Also Box 52900, Saxonwold, 2132, South Africa. Tel (011) 788 5549. Fax 788 6575. Telex 422302 SA.

Accommodation	*Facilities*	*Activities/ Attractions*
Camping	Licensed	Birdlife
Booking essential	Restaurant	Game viewing
	Shop	Mekoro hire
	Radio	Walks
	Camping equipment	Fishing

This is a camp into which you have to be flown, usually from Maun, which is quite an experience. The aerial views of the Delta are fascinating and, particularly in winter, offer a complete contrast from the barren dryness of the area around Maun. Travelling through the reed-lined waterways is a more intimate, personal experience of the Delta. Both the air and the boat trips are special in their own way. Neither is particularly comfortable, especially if you are suffering from the after-effects of the night before, so pick your partying time with care!

In its infancy Botswana's tourist industry was described as 'high cost low density'. Oddballs is part of the new wave 'low cost high density', where you can camp and then explore the Delta by mokoro. One of the less happy consequences of the flood of people into the Delta is that many of the campsites on some islands are festooned with fluttering ribbons of toilet paper and the debris of our throwaway society – to their great credit the management of Oddballs are meticulous in seeing that every bit of rubbish encountered in the sites they use is removed.

Oddballs' decor is quaint and original. The bar is built around a tall tree and leaky mekoro are given a new lease of life serving as ingenious cupboards.

Campers may come prepared with their own food and gear, although there is a shop where a limited range of tinned foods, clothing and curios can be bought. Self-catering chalets are also available.

POM POM CAMP Tariff: Medium
Kerr Downey & Selby, P O Box 40, Maun. Tel 660211-3. Fax 660379. Telex 2485 BD.

Accommodation	Facilities	Activities/ Attractions
Luxury tents	Licensed	Game walks
Booking essential	Restaurant	Game drives
	Radio	Fishing
	First Aid	Birdlife
		Boating
		Mekoro

This is a fly-in island camp in the heart of the permanent Delta. Part of the KDS group, it meets all their well-known standards for excellence and concern for client's needs.

From the hippo which inhabit the lagoon fronting the camp to the game that you'll encounter either by vehicle or on game walks, this camp presents a closeness to the Okavango and its inhabitants that you'll find hard to match.

Certainly, it is a wonderful place for the enthusiastic photographer. As with the Okavango generally, the bird life is enormously varied and plentiful and one does not have to be a 'bird' fanatic to enjoy this startling variety.

Being able to venture forth in a mokoro brings the Delta home to you in an intensely personal and unforgettable way.

SAN-TA-WANI Tariff: Medium
P O Box 100, Maun. Tel 660302. Telex 2648 BD.
Also Gametrackers, c/o Safariplan, Box 4245, Randburg, 2192, South Africa. Tel (011) 886 1810. Fax 886 1815.

Accommodation	Facilities	Activities/Attractions
Chalets	First aid	Birdlife
Booking essential – only through Gametrackers Safari Programmes	Licensed Radio	Game viewing Walks Game drives Canoes

San-ta-wani, one of the earlier lodges built in the Delta, is set among beautiful riverine trees. The buildings are of brick and thatch. Evening meals are served under the stars – weather permitting, which it usually does – in a reed-fenced boma. The chalets are spacious and each has an en suite toilet and a basin. Showers are a little distance away. In the chalets you will find a printed checklist of the area's birds, mammals and trees so that, if you are so inclined, you can have the satisfaction of recording your sightings. Clients are taken on game drives on request.

One of the special personalities at San-ta-wani is the blind gardener who lavishes such care on the plants that beautify the lodge. He is a favourite of many of the visitors and has been sent seeds from all over the world – a nightmare for those who have the responsibility of keeping the area free from alien, invader plants!

If you happen to be in San-ta-wani at full moon, ask one of the staff to take you to the nearby lagoon and there, on a silvered surface dotted with the brooding hulks of a hundred hippo, you will see reflected one of the most majestic moonrises that one could ask for.

SHINDE ISLAND Tariff: Medium
Kerr Downey & Selby, P O Box 40, Maun. Tel 660211/2/3. Fax 660379. Telex 2485 BD.

Accommodation	Facilities	Activities/Attractions
Luxury tents	Licensed	Game viewing
Booking essential	Restaurant	Fishing
	Radio	Birdlife
	First Aid	Boating
		Mekoro

This is another of the KDS luxury tented camps. Located in the region of the big river systems of the north-west, it is an island overlooking its own exclusive lagoon.

Typically, therefore, one will spend time in boats (both motor and mekoro), exploring the Delta and experiencing its wonders at first hand. There are plenty of opportunities to get out and walk on some of the bigger islands among the game.

A special feature of the area is that it tends to be favoured by the sitatunga antelope and there is a good chance that you may be lucky enough to catch a sighting of this elusive creature.

Boat trips to Gadikwe lagoon can show you breeding colonies of herons, egrets, comorants, pelicans and storks or, if you prefer, there is excellent fishing.

TSARO SAFARI Tariff: Medium

C/o Okavango Explorations, P O Box 69859, Bryanston, 2021, South Africa. Tel (011) 708 1893/5. Fax 708 1569. Telex 42 9795.

Accommodation	*Facilities*	*Activities/ Attractions*
Chalets	First aid	Birdlife
Booking essential	Licensed	Game viewing
	Swimming pool	Walks
	Shop	Game drives
	Radio	

Booking is essential and the lodge does not welcome casual visitors. Driving north over the pole bridge at the North Gate of Moremi, take the first main turning to the left. Some 5 km along this road you will see a white pump-house. Turn left and follow the track the remaining 1 km to the lodge.

Tsaro is graciously luxurious and quite different from the majority of lodges in the Delta. Here brick and mortar take the place of the more usual reeds and poles. The impression is of arriving at an elegant private home as a guest of the family – and that in fact is very much the ambience of Tsaro. Walk through the front door and your eye is drawn from a sparkling pool in a white-walled courtyard to a suspended mokoro, now no longer plying the waters of the Delta, but making an attractive plant container. The U-shaped courtyard opens onto a vista through shady trees, over lush green lawns, to the wild beyond.

Tucked unobtrusively to the side are the guests' chalets. No simple, round huts these, but of an intriguing split-level design where the bedroom looks down onto the sitting-room and the elegant bathroom has a sunken double bath. The camp accommodates a maximum of twelve clients at a time.

There is a shop with a small selection of clothes and curios, local artefacts, books and film.

Guests are taken out on early morning game drives and it is well worth the effort to follow the rhythm of the bush and rise just before the sun. Tsaro's game drives have many surprises to delight the receptive guest. Game walks are also offered, accompanied by a licensed, armed, professional guide. Birdwatching and boat excursions are a speciality and take place from a second camp at Xugana lagoon.

XAKANAXA Tariff: Medium
P/Bag 26, Maun. Tel 660222. Fax 660205. Telex 2482 BD.
Also P O Box 78304, Sandton, 2146, South Africa. Tel (011) 793 3957. Fax 793 1311.

Accommodation	Facilities	Activities/ Attractions
Chalets	First aid	Birdlife
Booking essential	Licensed	Game viewing
	Restaurant	Walks
	Radio	River cruises
		Game drives
		Fishing
		Flights
		Boating

One may fly in, by arrangement, from Maun or one may drive there. If you are driving, turn west, inside Moremi Reserve, just a short distance from North Gate. The distance to Xakanaxa lagoon is approximately 50 km. The route is signposted.

Xakanaxa is situated on the edge of the Xakanaxa lagoon, one of the most beautiful in the Delta. Under a canopy of giant trees, there is simple but comfortable accommodation for clients, who never number more than twelve, and who are treated to a taste of the real wild Africa.

Bird and game viewing trips can be organised to a client's taste and can be carried out on foot, by boat or vehicle. A speciality of this camp is to be found between the months of July and October. During this time there are large nesting colonies of marabou storks, open-bill and yellow-billed storks. Fishing in the lagoon is exciting and rewarding – providing one's concentration does not suffer from the repeated intrusions of curious but inoffensive hippo!

XAXABA CAMP Tariff: Medium
P O Box 100, Maun. Tel 660302. Telex 2648 BD.
Gametrackers, c/o Safariplan, Box 4245, Randburg, 2192, South Africa. Tel (011) 886 1810. Fax 886 1815.

Accommodation	Facilities	Activities/ Attractions
Chalets	Licensed	Birdlife
Booking essential	Swimming pool	Mekoro
	Shop	Walks
	Radio	River cruises
		Fishing
		Flights
		Boating

To get to this camp, deep in the Okavango Delta, you have to travel by air, usually from Maun. It is not a place for a casual drop-in as you pass. Booking is most important as Xaxaba is a very popular camp, especially during the busier months of the tourist season.

Xaxaba offers a range of facilities. These include boating, mokoro rides, fishing and walks through the incredibly beautiful flood-plains of the Delta. Aircraft flights can be arranged on request. A luxury camp of reed chalets is set in this 'place of tall trees', and as you wander through the camp you will see that the trees are discreetly identified, giving their common, scientific and Setswana names.

There is another camp, run by the same company, in the Delta. Known as Qhaaxwa (pronounced 'Kakwa'), it is located in the western Delta on the raised edge of an enormous lagoon, deep in a grove of shady trees. This beautiful spot epitomises the peace and tranquillity that is so typical of the Delta and it is well worth a visit.

Fishing is seasonally good, walks and boating can easily be arranged and the birdlife is outstanding. Accommodation at either of these camps is arranged through Xaxaba or their agents. A good idea is to combine, in one trip, a visit to both of these camps.

XUGANA Tariff: Medium

C/o Okavango Explorations, P O Box 69859, Bryanston, 2021, South Africa. Tel (011) 708 1893/5. Fax 708 1569. Telex 429795.

Accommodation	*Facilities*	*Activities/ Attractions*
Tented camp	First aid	Birdlife
Booking essential	Licensed	Game viewing
	Shop	Walks
	Radio	Cruises
		Game drives
		Fishing
		Flights
		Boating
		Water safaris

Access to Xugana is by air only. Note that weight restriction is 25 kg per person.

The lodge is on one of the largest lagoons in the Delta and a record catch of tiger fish has been made within hailing distance of the lodge's bar! Bream and catfish are also plentiful. All types of tackle are available at the lodge shop.

Xugana specialises in photographic tours. Many species of rare birds are found here, and the shy sitatunga is also seen in this area.

The Okavango Delta has attracted some of the world's celebrities. Xugana's most notable guest was Prince Charles, who spent several days at the lodge in 1984.

Savuti area

A fuller description of Savuti and its particular attractions is given on page 129. Here the landscape differs from that in the Moremi and Chobe. After pervading flatness, it is a pleasing change to see the hills in this area and there are Bushmen paintings to be found on some of the rocky outcrops.

Savuti can be very dry and you should carry water. The Savuti campsite suffers from the attention of elephant who have a habit of digging up the plumbing, leaving the campsite without water.

ALAN'S CAMP Tariff: Medium

P O Box 100, Maun. Tel 660302. Telex 2648 BD.
Also Gametrackers, c/o Safariplan, Box 4245, Randburg, 2192, South Africa. Tel (011) 886 1810. Fax 886 1815.

Accommodation	*Facilities*	*Activities/ Attractions*
Tented camp	First aid	Birdlife
Booking essential – only through Gametrackers Safari Programme	Licensed Radio	Game viewing Game drives

The chalets are A-frames built of local woods and have shower, basin and toilet en suite. The heart of the camp is a large tent where the cooking, eating, drinking and much yarning takes place.

Savuti can be an extremely dry area and the animals find the camps a gratuitous source of water – the septic tank is not immune from attack. The camp is tucked onto the bank of a bend in the channel, a good spot for game viewing. Game drives are arranged for clients. The frequent dryness of the surroundings does not make it the kind of place that appeals to all, so it is not a place to stay for any length of time unless you are one of the cognoscenti.

LINYANTI Tariff: High

P O Box 22, Kasane. Tel 250234. Telex 2763 BD.

Accommodation	*Facilities*	*Activities/ Attractions*
Tented camp	Licensed	Birdlife
Booking essential	Radio	Game viewing
	Gift shop	Walks
		Cruises
		Fishing

The Linyanti River forms the northern border between Botswana and the Caprivi Strip. There is a Department of Wildlife and National Parks public campsite on the river and some 20 km west is the lodge. Access is usually by air and the camp has its own airstrip.

The spacious tents that are the guest accommodation line the river bank and are set on lush green lawns. If your visit is in spring (late August, early September) the trees will be in blossom and the creamy trusses of knobthorn flowers are like an oriental painting against the deep blue sky. There is a short walk from tent to ablution block, which has showers and toilets. A portable basin is placed outside your tent each morning so that you can wash and not waste any birdwatching time!

The main building, housing dining-room and bar, is pole and thatch with an outside fireplace where the post-prandial ritual of coffee, liqueurs and tales of the bush occurs. One of the best places to sit and watch the world go by is on the upper deck of the double-decker barge which is used for game viewing. What a smooth, serene way to drift among the wildlife – and there is always the blissful option of a cold beer or drink for complete contentment.

LLOYD'S CAMP Tariff: Medium
P O Box 37, Maun.
Also P O Box 645, Bedfordview, 2008, South Africa. Tel (011) 453 7646. Fax 453 7648.

Accommodation	Facilities	Activities/ Attractions
Tented camp	First aid	Birdlife
Booking essential	Licensed	Game viewing
	Radio	Game drives
		Flights

Once you have reached the public campsite at Savuti, take any road that heads approximately west along the southern bank of the Savuti Channel. Lloyd's Camp is about 1 km from the public campsite. Lloyd will fly guests from Maun or Johannesburg to the camp.

If luxurious isolation from the wild is what you seek this is not the camp to visit. A *National Geographic* cover picture in 1983 was of Lloyd digging out a water-hole for a thirsty elephant standing within a trunk's touch. The photograph was taken just in front of the camp. It epitomises Lloyd's approach to wildlife – he believes in allowing his clients close encounters.

The camp is perched on the bank of the Savuti Channel and looks down onto what was the only source of surface water during the drought years of the early 1980s. There is a hide, where guests can sit unobtrusively, which commands a spectacular view of game visiting the water-hole. You can virtually count the vertebrae in an elephant's backbone. At night a spotlight is in constant use and many a guest has been held spellbound at a window, fascinated by the nightlife of the wild.

In this camp, of all the camps within the Okavango, one feels intimately a part of the turbulence, drama and beauty of Africa. During our visit we heard the panic-stricken squeals of a baboon troop as one of them was taken by a leopard not 100 m from where we lay sleeping. In the pre-dawn light we saw the silhouette of the predator and his prey high up in a tree. As the sun rose and more guests tore themselves from sleep to witness the drama, the leopard lithely dropped from the tree and melted away from our unwelcome attention.

SAVUTI SOUTH Tariff: Medium

P O Box 100, Maun. Tel 660302. Telex 2648 BD.
Also Gametrackers, c/o Safariplan, Box 4245, Randburg, 2192, South Africa. Tel (011) 886 1810. Fax 886 1815.

Accommodation	Facilities	Activities/ Attractions
Tented camp	First aid	Birdlife
Booking essential – only through Gametrackers Safari Programme	Licensed Radio	Game viewing Game drives

Savuti South was set up at a time when no permanent structures were allowed in National Parks, so both the communal area and the client accommodation are in tents. The blocks housing the showers, toilets and basins (built when the rule about no permanent structures was bent somewhat) are a short distance away from the tents – the significance of which will become clear. Savuti is 'big game' country and nocturnal visits to toilets are out of the question. Once the staff have escorted you to your tent at night, that is where you stay. Each tent is provided with a chamber pot, an essential part of the furniture.

Staying inside your tent is a wise precaution for the shadows abound with serious predators and thirsty elephants. On one occasion we were quietly watching the darkness after the rest of the camp had gone to bed. Virtually immediately after the last guest had been escorted from the main area, three distinctive shadows insinuated themselves around the bird-bath in front of the main tent. So suddenly did they appear that we were sure the hyena family had been waiting in the dark right at the edge of the companionable circle of people around the fire.

Almost like a stage performance where the players assemble in the dark of an uncurtained stage before the lights go up, an elephant was right there within metres of us. We had heard not one hint of his arrival – but felt that the pounding of our hearts was letting the whole world know, elephant, hyena and all, that we were there and terrified.

The drama proceeded with a sudden cacophony of metal on metal on more metal. It sounded as if every metal implement in the kitchen tent was being thrown and bashed and pounded together. Suspense was now added to terror. What could possibly make that amount of noise? We had to wait for the morning to establish that it was merely the nightly visit of the hyena to the rubbish bin!

SELINDA BUSH CAMP Tariff: High
P O Box 22, Kasane. Tel 250234. Telex 2763 BD.

Accommodation	Facilities	Activities/ Attractions
Luxury tents	Radio	Exclusive
	Licensed	Game walks
		Game drives
		Birds

This remarkable camp forms part of a trio run by Brian and Jan Graham, the owners of Linyanti Explorations; their other camps are Chobe Chilwero and Linyanti.

In the last ten years we have watched Brian's enterprises grow slowly and succeed enormously. They have done so because of his unremitting commitment to quality, service and efficiency. Everything he and Jan do is stamped with their personal hallmark of real quality and extraordinarily high standards.

These you will find reflected in the exclusive six-bed tented camp at Selinda. Each tent has its own private shower and toilet. We can assure you, you will not find better.

The camp is located in a fascinating area. Less than a kilometre away is the exit point on the Linyanti (Chobe) river from which the famed Savuti Channel leaves, in those years when it mysteriously choses to flow. Equally enigmatic in its unpredictable flow patterns is the Selinda Spillway, which also enters the Linyanti near here.

This is big game country and there are few animals occurring in Botswana that you will not find here as, in the care of professionals, you drive of walk amongst them.

Nata area

Until recently, virtually the only reason for stopping at Nata was to refuel. Now there are interesting additional reasons. With the establishment of the Sua Pan Bottle-store, just about any exotic taste in alcohol can be indulged. The owner makes sure that in the tourist season he stocks a wide range of liquor, from French wines and British ciders to exotic liqueurs. The enterprising owner also offers good quality meals – and his chips are the best in this part of Africa! The new bottle-store is an indication of how local entrepreneurs see the potential of the tourist business.

A further attraction in the area is Nata Lodge.

NATA LODGE Tariff: Budget
P/Bag 10, Francistown. Tel & Fax 611210.

Accommodation	Facilities	Activities/ Attractions
4-Bed furnished safari tents	Airstrip at Nata	Birdlife Swimming pool
Chalets	First aid	4 × 4 excursions
Camping	Licensed	to Makgadi-
Booking essential during the holiday season	Restaurant Shop Petrol Diesel	kgadi pans

Nata Lodge is some 10 km south of Nata on the main tar road from Francistown, and is well situated as a stop-over point for visitors to Maun, the Delta, Chobe National Park, Victoria Falls and Zambia. It is clearly signposted – so keep your eyes open for the distinctive logo of the helmeted guineafowl.

The attractive A-framed cottages, each with a private shower and toilet, stand among tall ilala palms, marula and monkey thorn trees. The site is near the north-eastern edge of the great Makgadikgadi Pans, an area of unique beauty.

In times of good rains, this portion of the pan floods and might retain an initial metre or more of water for several years. At such times, flamingo, pelican and other water birds appear in tens of thousands.

To deal with the thirst that builds up on a long journey, the lodge has a bar – inside for the chill winter evenings, outside at the large swimming pool to beat the summer heat. There is also a restaurant with an à la carte and a 'snack' menu.

The area generally is considered to be excellent for birdwatching – mainly because of the diversity of habitats close to the lodge.

Campers are particularly welcome here also, and there are brick and thatched ablution blocks – with lots of hot and cold water to emphasise that welcome, all in a cool and shady campsite.

Tuli area

Tuli is an area of Botswana that deserves far more attention than it gets at present. It lies to the east of the Kalahari sands and the rocky landscape is full of interesting hills and valleys. This is also an area of great historical and archaeological interest. It is rich in game and the nature of the landscape is such that game viewing is much facilitated.

JWALA GAME LODGE Tariff: Budget
P/Bag X1040, Waterpoort, 0905, South Africa.
Also P O Box 52023, Saxonwold, 2132, South Africa. Tel (011) 7880741.
Fax 880 6244.

Accommodation	Facilities	Activities/ Attractions
Bush camps	First aid	Birdlife
Booking essential	Dining-room	Game viewing
		Walks
		Game drives
		Trails

Travelling from Johannesburg, take the road to Pont Drift where you will pass through Customs and Immigration. If you go via Pietersburg and Alldays, the journey takes about 6 hours. The border post closes at 4 pm. An alternative is to fly into Tuli Lodge where Customs and Immigration formalities can be dispensed with, and then to the Jwala Game Lodge airstrip.

Jwala Lodge has a range of facilities. There are two fully self-contained bush camps, each accommodating ten people. Both have hot and cold showers, flush toilets, thatched kitchen areas and fridges.

All around the lodge and its garden one is aware of an artist's touch – weavings made using bark and elephant droppings, polished driftwood sculptures, and all kinds of *objets d' art* gathered from the veld and produced by the local weavers.

The special ambience of Jwala is created by the Petty family, who opted out of urban living and conventional careers to realise a dream. They are your hosts and will take you on game drives or walks through the area.

MASHATU GAME RESERVE Tariff: High
P O Box 2575, Randburg, 2125, South Africa. Tel (011) 789 2677. Telex 4-24807 SA. (Note: all bookings must be made through travel agents in Botswana or through the address given above.)

Accommodation	Facilities	Activities/ Attractions
Luxury chalets	Licensed	Game drives
Luxury tents	Private bar	Game Walks
Booking essential	Fully catered	Night drives
	Swimming pools	Birdwatching
	Conference room	

Located in the north-east Tuli Block, the Reserve's closest border crossing into South Africa is at Pontdrift. Fly-in facilities are available and customs and immigration clearance at the airfield can be arranged when booking.

Air charter and fly-in packages can be booked either in Johannesburg or in Gaborone. Driving time from Johannesburg is 5–6 hours via Pietersburg and Alldays. The driving time from Gaborone is much the same.

It is important to remember that the border closes at 4.00 pm. Self-drive guests are met at the border by game reserve staff and transported to the camps.

Mashatu is the largest privately owned conservation area in Southern Africa. The area has a remarkable diversity of landscape and wildlife, and its elephants, particularly, are well known. Other large animals to be found there include lion, leopard, cheetah, giraffe and many of the antelopes. There are two commercial camps at Mashatu.

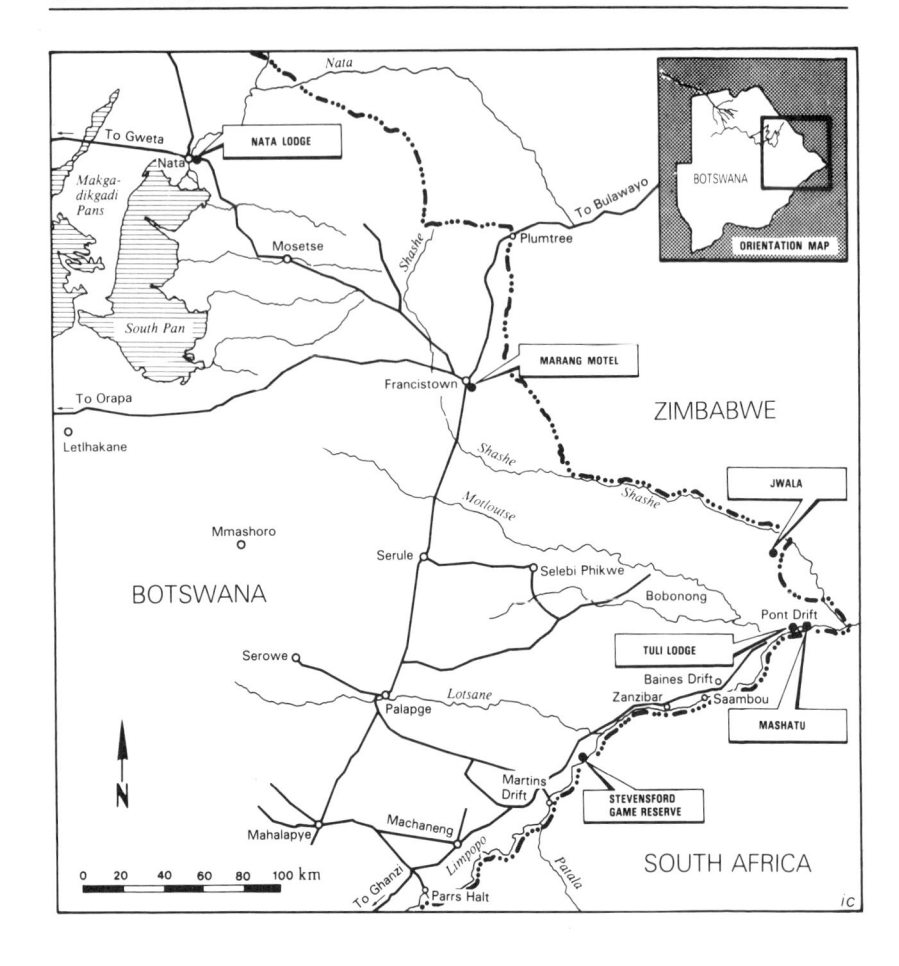

Majale Camp accommodates a maximum of thirty guests in luxuriously appointed air-conditioned rondavels and chalets. The camp has recently been completely renovated and makes an ideal venue for corporate clientele and senior management seminars as well as catering for the needs of foreign and local travellers who enjoy a certain amount of luxury during their bushveld holiday.

A feature of the camp is a thatched observation bar overlooking a floodlit waterhole. There is a filtered swimming pool. Day and night game drives are conducted in open four-wheel-drive vehicles and walking tours, led by experienced rangers, are also offered.

Thakadu Camp is a luxury tented camp accommodating a maximum of 14 guests. The character of the camp is entirely rustic, although every convenience is available to guests. Features of the camp are its very personalised atmosphere and the aura of wilderness which prevails. There is a swimming pool and game outings are conducted in the same manner as at Majale.

STEVENSFORD GAME RESERVE Tariff: Budget
P O Box 26, Sherwood Ranch *or* c/o Phuti Travel, P/Bag 00297, Gaborone. Tel 314166. Fax 374290. Telex 2521 BD.

Accommodation	Facilities	Activities/ Attractions
Chalets	First aid	Birdlife
Booking essential	Swimming pool	Game viewing
	Radio telephone	Walks
		Game drives
		Fishing
		Boating
		Horse-riding
		Bicycles

After crossing the border into Botswana at Groblersbrug/Martins Drift and driving a further 8 km, turn right at Sherwood Ranch, onto the Baines Drift road. Fourteen kilometres along this road is a well-signposted entrance to the reserve.

The camp is built in a beautiful riverine habitat, close to the banks of the Limpopo River. Accommodation is provided in thatched, rondavel-type chalets – three with bathroom en suite and two with outside ablution facilities. Four of the chalets have four beds each and the other has two beds.

Clients are advised to provide all their own consumables and bedding, although bedding can be obtained at a nominal charge. All other equipment, eg crockery, fridge, freezer etc, is provided.

Stevensford Game Reserve is open all year round and is very popular. A special feature is that a block booking of six or more people can claim exclusive use of the reserve and its facilities. There are several hides from which to view and photograph game and birds, while horse-riding through the bush is an unforgettable experience. The reasonable daily rate is inclusive of all the facilities, including game drives and the use of bicycles. There are no extra charges.

Tswana Safaris Tariff: Budget
P O Box 5, Sherwood Ranch. Tel 846212.

Accommodation	Facilities	Activities/ Attractions
Thatched cottage	No Licence	Game drives
Your own tents	No restaurant	Game walks
(September to	Telephone	Birdlife
April only)	First aid	

This ramarkable and tiny camp is definately one that should not be overlooked. Managed by Roy and Charlotte Young, it lies on one of the large Tuli block estates.

The estate is given over to game ranching and, during the season, to hunting, when it is closed to non-hunting clients. Between September and April, however, it is open to groups of up to six persons (more if you are prepared to camp).

The lucky group gets the complete seclusion and isolation of this enchanted Limpopo riverine habitat. The comfortable chalet is only for those who wish to cater for themselves and so you need to bring all your own supplies. However, the rates are extremely reasonable and so this makes for a good, inexpensive family holiday.

Children are welcome and everyone is free to roam wherever they chose. On a ranch well stocked with every kind of antelope, including gemsbok and eland, as well as impala, wildebeest and many others, this freedom and the absence of predators makes for a memorable and tension free 'get-away'.

Tuli Lodge Tariff: Medium
P O Box 945, Gaborone. Also P O Box 41478, Craighall, 2024, South Africa. Tel (011) 788 1748/9. Fax 788 6804.

Accommodation	Facilities	Activities/ Attractions
Chalets	Licensed	Birdlife
Booking essential	Swimming pool	Game viewing
	Luxury conference venue	Walks
		Game drives

Clients can fly into Tuli Lodge from Lanseria near Johannesburg, or they can drive there. For the fly-in guests Customs facilities are organised by the lodge.

If approaching from South Africa, drive to Pont Drift. The lodge is about 7 km from the border in a westerly direction. About 2 km beyond the border there is a road to the left signposted 'Tuli lodge'.

Vehicles can safely be left at the border post and guests will be transferred by Tuli Lodge vehicles. One can drive through but it is not advisable due to the road surfaces and the possibility, at any time during the summer months, of the Limpopo coming down in flood.

(If the river should flood – you can enjoy, in this Star Wars/Computer century in which we live, the thrill of being hauled across a raging flooded African river in a wire cage suspended on a steel hawser! It's great fun and perfectly safe.)

The best route from Gaborone is Mahalapye–Palapye–Martins Drift–Zanzibar–Tuli. This is about 514 km.

From Francistown the best route is via Selebi–Phikwe–Bobonong, but the road is not always in good condition.

As the most popular time to visit the wildlife areas of Botswana is winter, when the bush is dry, dusty and brown, Tuli Lodge makes a most dramatic impression. Visitors think they have arrived at an oasis. At any time of year the garden is breathtaking. Its design is bold and the effect a beautiful, harmonious blend of indigenous trees and all manner of plants.

The buildings have also been sensitively designed to blend and complement the setting – the bar embraces a tree, and the dining-room seems to be part of the garden with its etched glass panels protecting but not separating one from the world around.

Apart from merely relaxing in the beauty of the surroundings, guests are also taken on game drives. The sparkling swimming pool is an attraction for the energetic or the sun worshipper.

Western Delta area

The western part of the Delta is the place for fishing enthusiasts and several fishing camps have been established here. This is the home of Botswana's famous basket-makers. It is a fascinating adventure to visit villages such as Nokaneng, Gomare and Etsha, and to meet the basket-makers there. It requires time and patience, but the effort can be rewarded with some really special baskets.

Two other attractions of the Western Delta are the Tsodilo Hills and Drotsky's Cave. Full details about these places are given in Chapter 1. A quick way through the Caprivi Strip is also described in that section.

ETSATSA Tariff: High
P/Bag 013, Maun. Tel 660302. Fax 660351. Telex 2612 BD *or* Tel (011) 979 1264.

Accommodation	Facilities	Activities/Attractions
Luxury tents	Radio	Fishing
	Catering	Mekoro trails
	Full bar	Island walks
		Birdwatching

One of the unsung gems of the Okavango – and there are many of them yet to come to light – is this superb camp on an island near the foot of the panhandle – where it begins to spread out into the Delta proper.

Essentially a fisherman's camp, it is not exclusively so, for the range of activities offered is wide.

Perhaps its single greatest attraction is the atmosphere of warmth, welcome and genuine hospitality extended by Geoff Randall and his wife Nookie. They attend to practically everything personally – which explains the high per centage of repeat business they enjoy.

The accommodation is comfortable and the tents roomy and well maintained. Each has its own ablution facilities including wonderful showers and a flush toilet.

Remote Etsatsa is most usually approached by air (to Seronga village). The island is right on the edge of the open river. It caters for a maximum of 16 persons and the daily rate includes all meals, drinks (except wine) and excursions – even lost fishing tackle.

FISH EAGLE LODGE Tariff: Medium
P/Bag 13, Maun. Tel 660351. Fax 660571. Telex 2612 BD.

Accommodation	Facilities	Activities/Attractions
A-frame chalets	First aid	Fishing
Reed huts	Licensed	Birdlife
Houseboat	Radio	Boating
Camping		Boat hire

Probably among the most distant from Maun of the Okavango lodges, Drotsky's, as Fish Eagle Lodge is sometimes called, after its owners, can be reached by the ever-progressing tar as it continually extends up the western side of the Delta, but most people arrive by air.

If you are into fishing on the big rivers of the Okavango, this is the place for you, for the camp overlooks the main river as it flows down the 100 km of the panhandle.

There is a choice of very comfortable accommodation and the rates are exceedingly moderate. Five-metre powerboats are available for daily or hourly hire so this is an ideal opportunity for independent travellers visiting the western Delta by road to take a day or two off, camp and explore the waterways.

A unique aspect of this camp is the opportunity to hire a houseboat (minimum of six people) and spend time out in some of the remotest parts of the Delta.

JEDIBE ISLAND CAMP Tariff: High
P/Bag 14, Maun, *or* Box 651171, Benmore, 2010, South Africa. Tel (011) 884 1458/9. Fax 883 6255. Telex 42 8642.

Accommodation	*Facilities*	*Activities/ Attractions*
Tented chalets	Bar	Birdwatching
Mekoro camping trails	Restaurant	Game viewing
	Radio	Mekoro trails
Booking essential		Boating
		Fishing

The island is located in the centre of that portion of the Okavango which has water all the year round. The annual variation in water level is little more than 35 cm!

There are no roads here and no vehicles. Jedibe is strictly a water experience. The two main activities are mekoro and boating to allow guests access to two very different habitats in the area.

To the north-east of the camp are the big rivers and large open expanses of water. Elsewhere, the flood plains are accessible only by mekoro.

Walks under the supervision of licensed professional guides are undertaken on the larger islands.

The area is one of the best in Botswana for Pel's fishing owl and there is a resident pair in the camp. You can also expect to find pygmy geese, swamp boubou shrike, western banded snake eagle, Heuglin's robin and slaty egrets.

As far as game is concerned, you can expect to see buffalo, hippo, crocodile, sitatunga and red lechwe.

NXAMASERI FISHING CAMP Tariff: Medium
P/Bag 23, Maun. Tel & Fax 660493. Telex 2482 BD.

Accommodation	Facilities	Activities/ Attractions
Chalets	First aid	Birdlife
Booking essential	Licensed	Game viewing
	Restaurant	Walks
	Radio	River cruises
		Fishing
		Flights
		Boating

It is possible to drive to this camp but it is a long, uncomfortable journey, despite the tarring of the road which will soon have passed the vicinity of this lovely water camp. It is more usual for clients to fly from Maun and this can be arranged when you book.

Nxamaseri is a very popular fishing camp in a beautiful setting on the western side of the Delta.

Accommodation is in the small, intimate camp set among giant riverine trees. The greenness of the area contrasts vividly with the aridity of the surroundings, particularly if you visit in the dry months of May to November. Water-lilies and the reflections of reeds give an almost surreal, three-dimensional effect. Nxamaseri is Mecca for the fisherman or birdwatcher and the camp's intimate, friendly atmosphere is an added attraction.

To add diversity to its product and to offer a better service to its clients, Nxamaseri makes use of another nearby location. This is the Guma Lagoon – a place, in its way, as charming and memorable as Nxamaseri itself.

If you are interested in the unusual, and horses, you might ask the owners of Nxamaseri to tell you something about their pioneering long-distance horse safaris in the western delta.

Shakawe Fishing Camp/Okavango Fishing Safaris Tariff: Medium

P O Box 12, Shakawe. Tel & Fax (Maun) 660493. Telex 2487 BD.

Accommodation	Facilities	Activities/Attractions
Chalets	First aid	Birdlife
Camping	Licensed	Walks
Booking advisable	Swimming pool	Fishing
	Radio	Boating
	Meals (on request)	Tsodilo Hills

It is possible to drive to Shakawe from Maun, but the road is 370 km of heavy sand and the journey is not recommended. Shakawe is accessible by charter aircraft from all main centres to which schedule flights operate, and Shakawe airfield has Customs and Immigration facilities. A collection fee is charged by the camp.

The camp, one of the first tourist camps in Botswana, is perched on a high bank, overlooking a bend in the Okavango River. Birdwatching is outstanding, owing to the wide range of habitats (riverine bush, savannah and semi-desert) in a small area.

The campsite also overlooks the river and there are ablution blocks with hot and cold showers and flush toilets.

A tented camp of large cottage tents is located under magnificent trees. Each tent has its own toilet facilities.

Clients are catered for but campers must be self-sufficient. Fish can usually be bought from local fishermen.

The best time for fishing is from April to November. The bream are good in June and July and the best time for taking on the fighting tiger fish is from August to October.

The camp will organise vehicle excursions to Tsodilo Hills and the fascinating Nxamaseri Valley. Depending on the state of the road, the journey to the Hills takes about four hours. The San (Bushmen) who live in the area sell a small range of curios. River cruises are also available.

Xaro Lodge Tariff: High

P/Bag 14, Maun. Tel & Fax 660632. Also P O Box 651171, Benmore, 2010, South Africa. Tel 884 1458/883 5617. Fax 883 6255. Telex 4-28642 SA.

Accommodation	Facilities	Activities/ Attractions
Luxury double tents	Licensed	Birdlife
Booking essential	Radio	Limited game viewing
		Walks
		River cruises
		Fishing
		Flights
		Boating
		Tsodilo Hills

The only way to get to this camp, situated on the western side of the Delta's panhandle, is to fly. Bookings include all the necessary air travel arrangements, whether the visitor is arriving from an international starting point or beginning his journey in Maun.

Xaro Lodge is, primarily, a camp with the fisherman in mind. It is situated on a peninsula which juts out into the Okavango River and captures the mood of the ever-changing, fast-flowing river. Xaro is renowned for the most exciting and challenging fishing in the Delta.

In addition to its fishing, Xaro Lodge also offers remarkable opportunities for birdwatchers. A pair of Pel's fishing owls regularly hunts in front of the camp and, in the season, nesting African skimmers, white-backed herons and fish eagles are among the many attractions. Game can also be seen in the vicinity of the camp, including hippo, crocodile, as well as the rare sitatunga antelope.

An interesting and unusual facility offered by Xaro are trips by vehicle or by air to nearby Tsodilo Hills. Here there are more than 2 500 rock paintings and the area is still inhabited by San. All safaris conducted by Xaro are led by experienced and professional guides.

Accommodation at the camp, which never takes more than sixteen guests at a time, is in luxury double tents equipped with beds, electric lights, and cupboards. Attractive African rugs brighten up the décor. There is a modern and well-equipped bathroom adjacent to each pair of tents. The dining-room, lounge and well-stocked bar are focal points of the camp and are all constructed in typical African style, under thatch.

CAMPSITES IN NATIONAL PARKS

The days when one could simply pull off the road and make camp are almost a thing of the past. The increase in human and cattle populations – the latter has trebled in the twenty years since Independence in 1966 – means that, other than in the very remote parts of the country, you are unlikely to be alone.

Campsites in Botswana are either privately owned or administered by the Department of Wildlife and National Parks. All the privately owned campsites are attached to lodges and have been included in the description of the individual lodges. The map on page 100 indicates campsite locations.

Chobe National Park

Chobe boasts five campsites.

Savuti

A stay at Savuti campsite seems to be on the itinerary of every four-wheel-drive vehicle. Sadly, the amount of rubbish left lying around and the state of the roads testify to this. This is probably the only place where you need to use a four-wheel-drive vehicle just to get into your campsite. Although there are toilet and shower facilities, pumps are often not working or thirsty elephants have rearranged the plumbing.

Savuti Channel in the seventies was a place of hippos and water. Throughout the eighties, however, it has been very dry. It is still a fine place to see game of all kinds, which is part of the reason for its popularity.

Take care not to keep fruit, especially oranges, in your tent or vehicle as this can focus the unwanted attention of elephant on you.

Linyanti

The Linyanti campsite is on the banks of the Linyanti river and looks into the Caprivi Strip. Although it does have shower and toilet facilities, the same provisos apply here as for all the other camps – don't rely on them being operational.

Linyanti is a little bit off the beaten track and consequently appeals to those who prefer their wilderness to be more private.

Nogatsaa

This was clearly quite a substantial camp in days gone by. There is a large dam with a sturdily constructed hide overlooking the water. There are huts but they are not available for hire at present. There are also toilets and showers. Some game guards are resident at Nogatsaa.

That highly regarded doyen of safari operators in Botswana, Colin Bell of Okavango Wilderness Safaris, has passed on to me a useful tip about the water supply at this camp.

There is a borehole, says Colin, and the problem is not so much the lack of water but an absence of diesel with which to drive the pump! He recommends carrying the odd litre or two as there will be no objections to your using the pump if you can produce the diesel!

Tjinga/Tshinga/Tchinga

However you spell it, this is a pleasing campsite. There is a water tank on a tall stand and a pump to get the water up to that tank – a welcome sight at the end of a hot, dry, dusty journey. Other than this there are no facilities.

If you have a mechanical bent you will probably get the pump going in a jiffy. Failing that, there might be some expert camping there already who will kindly show you how it is done. If neither of these options is available it is going to be an initiative test. As a clue, by dint of yanking on the drive belt – having ensured that there is fuel in the motor – when the parts are moving, push the switch down and pray for that 'chug-chug' that heralds action. If none of these work for you, your consolation will have to be in knowing just how wonderful *we* found our Tjinga shower!

The advice of Colin Bell about carrying a small quantity of diesel (see first paragraph of this page) is also applicable here.

Serondela

Serondela is on the itinerary of every four-wheel-drive vehicle *and* every two-wheel-drive vehicle that passes through the area. You will be lucky to find a quiet spot tucked away somewhere. If not, you will have to accept that if you are there in high season you will have many neighbours.

There are toilets and showers here which usually work. They are also usually unpleasant when battling to cope with more people than they were designed for.

Moremi Wildlife Reserve

South Gate

This campsite, set among mopani trees, is just outside the reserve and is generally only used by people who have arrived after the gate closes. Although there are toilets, there is no guarantee that the pump will be working. You may have to draw water from the well and use 'long-drop' toilets. Showers are available.

Third Bridge

This is probably the most popular campsite in Moremi and in peak season is extremely crowded. Pure pressure of people has forced the Department of Wildlife and National Parks to provide some kind of facilities, and 'long-drop' toilets in shoulder-high log enclosures have been put in. Water is available from the river and it is a pleasant place to swim. Showers are available.

Should you see anyone lathering themselves with soap and preparing to wash off in the water, do encourage them to do their rinsing on the banks so that the beautiful clear water remains just so.

Xakanaxa

In the old days, when maps of the area did not exist, it was quite a challenge to find this magical spot. It is a great deal easier nowadays, although the trade-off is that you may have to share it with the world and his wife. There are currently no facilities here at all. A number of safari operators have camps here and you may be able to hire a boat from the operators.

North Gate

This campsite lies just within the reserve and has shower and toilet facilities, as well as an ample supply of water – under normal conditions. What is not always guaranteed is that the pump will be working.

Nxai Pan National Park

Apart from the informal campsites at Baines' Baobabs, there are two campsites in Nxai Pan National Park. From the main entrance drive about 7 km to the edge of the pan. The first site is on the southern edge of the pan, some 3 km from the game scouts' camp.

The second camp is on the northern edge of the pan, about 6 km beyond the game scouts' camp. Although toilet and shower facilities are provided, there is no guarantee that they will be working. Often the game scouts are without a vehicle so servicing the tourist camps is something of a problem.

Makgadikgadi Game Reserve

There is a campsite in this reserve, on the Boteti River opposite the village of Xhumaga. The setting is lovely and is enhanced by the presence of a toilet and shower (cold water only at the moment – but hot is to come) and a stand pipe offering fresh water.

Firewood is said to be available – but bring your own just in case. A deep rubbish pit exists, (but we would rather take our rubbish out with us – such pits are seldom managed as they should be.)

MOBILE SAFARI OPERATORS

If you are not able to provide your own transport for exploring Botswana, or if you prefer to take advantage of others' expertise to take you off the beaten track, there are a number of operators who run mobile safaris in Botswana.

A mobile safari is a commercial safari operation which moves from place to place by boat, vehicle or both, camping in the bush or using the facilities offered by some of the fixed camps or national park campsites.

Starting points

There are basically two categories of starting point, those outside Botswana and those within. The closer you can get to your main area of interest under your own steam, the cheaper the safari hire is going to be.

The main starting points in Botswana are Gaborone, Kasane and Maun.

There is a good quality tarred road to Gaborone and Kasane and any reasonable car can get there from South Africa, Zimbabwe and Zambia. Maun can only be reached from Nata, the track from Kasane via the Savuti or from the borders with Namibia. The road from Nata is presently being tarred; the others vary in condition depending upon the time of the year and how recently graders have been in action. Basically, any big two-wheel-drive vehicle can get from Nata to Maun, providing you stay on the hard surface and don't move down into the verges. The road is wide enough to take two lanes of traffic but is normally used by very heavy trucks which cause a lot of dust, throw up stones and cause serious corrugations at times.

One would not normally try to get to Maun from Namibia without a four-wheel-drive vehicle, although VW Kombis and Peugeots do get through in the dry season.

Trying to keep abreast of so mobile a population as mobile safari operators in Botswana is a daunting undertaking!

In looking around for the operators to help up-date this guide the first 'mobile safari' we encountered was really something of a surprise. Although it was mobile it definitely was not what we had in mind, for we had stumbled on Botswana's new and exciting *elephant* safaris. This amazing experience offers you the unforgettable opportunity to travel in the Okavango Delta on the back of a trained African elephant!

However, as we said, this was not the sort of mobile operator we had in mind (but if you are interested you can find out more from Safari South, P O Box 40, Maun. Tel 660211-3, Fax 660379, Tx 2485 BD) and so we had to look further afield.

Because of the changes that take place among the many operators, we have adopted a somewhat different approach from the first edition in presenting information on this group to you.

Below is a list, with addresses and contact numbers, of all the well-known and reputable mobile safari operators known to us. It includes those based in Botswana as well as in neighbouring countries.

In brackets, after each name, there appears a figure which indicates the number of years the operator or his company has been in business. (In the case of that wonderful man, Izak Barnard, who has been doing safaris in Africa for longer than many of us have been around, we've limited ourselves to a polite upper limit of '+20'!)

After this we have listed a series of variables which you need to consider before making a final decision as to which operator you intend to choose. These variables have a strong influence on the cost of the safari you are planning.

We suggest that, after considering these, you contact your own travel agent, or one of those listed on pages 165–166 and let their recommendations guide you to the final choice. After all, the agents are right on the spot, expecially those in Maun, and most certainly know what is going on in the mobile safari business.

List of known Mobile Safari Operators

(All of whose Botswana staff are understood to hold Professional Guides Licences.)

Africa Calls (10)	P/Bag 13, Maun, Botswana. Tel 660614
Afroventures (20)	P O Box 2339, Randburg, 2125, South Africa. Tel (011) 789 1078. Fax 886 2349 P O Box 55, Kasane, Botswana. Tel 250456. Fax 250223. Tx 2763 BD
Bhati Safaris (15)	Box 651171, Benmore, 2010, South Africa. Tel (011) 884 1458/9. Fax 883 6255 P/Bag 14, Maun, Botswana. Tel & Fax 660632

Bushdrifters (8)	P O Box 785743, Sandton, 2146, South Africa. Tel (011) 659 1551/2. Fax 659 1122. Tx 4-30753 SA
Capricorn Safari (7)	P/Bag 21, Maun, Botswana. Tel 660351. Fax 660571. Tx 2612 BD
Crocodile Camp Safaris (7)	Box 46, Maun, Botswana. Tel 660265. Fax 660493. Tx 2487 BD
Daphne Wilmot Safaris (3)	P/Bag 13, Maun, Botswana. Tel 660351/571. Fax 660571. Tx 2612 BD
Drifters (8)	P O Box 48434, Roosevelt Park, 2129, South Africa. Tel (011) 486 1224. Fax 486 1237
Go Wild (3)	P O Box 56, Kasane, Botswana. Tel 250237. Fax 250223. Tx 2763 BD
Gweta Safari Lodge (4)	P O Box 124, Gweta, Botswana. P O Box 236, Maun, Botswana. Tel & Fax 660493. Tx 2487 BD
Kalahari-Kavango Safaris (8)	P O Box 236, Maun, Botswana. Tel & Fax 660493. Tx 2487 BD
Karibu Safari (+10)	P/Bag 39, Maun, Botswana. Box 35196, Northway, Durban, 4065, South Africa. Tel (031) 83 9774. Fax 83 1957. Telex 6-23026 SA
Kitso Safari (8)	P O Box 236, Maun, Botswana. Tel & Fax 660493. Tx 2487 BD
Koro Safari (20)	P/Bag 11, Maun, Botswana. Tel 660430. Fax 660307. Tx 2618 BD
Nata Lodge (6)	P/Bag 10, Francistown, Botswana. Tel & Fax 611210
NRS Tours (2)	Phuti Travel, Gaborone. Tel 314166 or write to P O Box 59, Tsabong, Botswana
Okavango Wilderness Safaris (+10)	Box 651171, Benmore, 2010, South Africa. Tel (011) 884 1458/9. Fax 883 6255 P/Bag 14, Maun, Botswana. Tel & Fax 660632.
Okuti (+8)	P.Bag 049, Maun. Tel & Fax 660307. Tx 2618 BD

Papadi Safaris (6)	P O Box 3684, Honeydew, 2040, South Africa. Tel (011) 679 3525. Fax 475 5369. Tx 425046 SA
Penduka Safaris (+20)	P O Box 55413, Northlands, 2116, South Africa. Tel & Fax (011) 883 4303
Penstone Safaris (15)	P O Box 330, Maun, Botswana. Tel & Fax 660520. Tx 2612 BD. P O Box 52900, Saxonwold, 2132, South Africa. Tel (011) 788 5549. Fax 788 6575
Soren Lindstrom (20)	P/Bag 13, Maun, Botswana. Tel 660351. Fax 660571. Tx 2612 BD
Southern Cross Safari (+10)	P/Bag 11, Maun, Botswana. Tel 660430. Fax 660307. Tx 2618 BD
Wildlife Safaris (2)	P O Box 236, Maun, Botswana. Tel & Fax 660493. Tx 2487 BD

If you are considering mobile operators for want of your own 4 × 4 and the necessary equipment that goes with it, you may be interested to know of Bushlink. They are a Botswana company that hires out fully equipped 4 × 4s with everything from crockery to cutlery to bedding and chairs. Their vehicles appear to be well looked after and their equipment of good quality. They operate from both Gaborone and Kasane and can be contacted at:

Bushlink: Mr & Mrs Lyall, P/Bag 00314, Gaborone, Botswana. Tel & Fax 371480.

Factors affecting Price

When you plan to travel with a mobile operator there are various aspects that you will need to consider. Use the list of factors below to help you make your choices. Discuss them with a travel agent who is experienced in this field. The nature of your choices will affect the price.

Do it yourself or full service	The degree to which you are prepared to physically participate in the day-to-day chores of safari life is a considerable factor influencing cost.
Level of service	Some companies ask you to 'help here and there', others want you to do nothing, while some go to the extreme of pampering you as in the great and fabled East African Safaris of an (almost) forgotten luxurious era.
Ready made vs tailor-made packages	Whether the safari is a standard package or whether it is tailored to your precise requirements.
Number of days	
Number of people	
Distance travelled	
Places visited	You pay extra for visiting expensive places, like Chobe National Park and Moremi Game Reserve. You also pay for exclusivity and for complete privacy.
Company's reputation	You can expect to pay a little more for the security of a good reputation based on many years of good service.
Guide's reputation	Sometimes there is a premium for the leader or guide whom you might wish to have lead you.
Add on extras	Such things as a flight above the Victoria Falls, or an extra trip by mokoro may not be part of the 'package'. Try to check these.
Speciality tours	Often the price of the safari is influenced by specialised purposes. For instance, a horseback trail, birding, photography, etc.

8. MISCELLANEOUS INFORMATION

AIRCRAFT CHARTER AND MAINTENANCE

Air Charter

Maun

Aer-Kavango	P O Box 169, Maun. Tel & Fax 660393. Fax only 660507. Telex 2759 BD.
Air Xaxaba	P O Box 147, Maun. Tel 660302. Fax 660571. Telex 2648 BD.
Elgon Air	P O Box 448, Maun. Tel 660351. Fax 660571.
Wildlife Helicopters	P/Bag 161, Maun. Tel & Fax 660664.
Northern Air	P O Box 40, Maun. Tel 660385/211/2/3. Fax 660379. Telex 2485 BD.

Gaborone

Executive Air	P/Bag SK6, Gaborone. Tel 375257. Fax 375258
Kalahari Air Services & Charter	P O Box 41278, Broadhurst, Gaborone. Tel 351804/353593. Fax 312015. Telex 2502 BD.
Western Air	P O Box 40763, Gaborone. Tel & Fax 373386. Tel 353609.

Aircraft Maintenance

There are two aircraft maintenance businesses in Botswana.

In Gaborone, Kalahari Air Services and Charter offer full servicing for all types of aircraft, including jets. Servicing ranges from routine maintenance to 50, 100 and 2 000 hour servicing and re-builds.

In Maun, a general maintenance service is offered by Northern Air, this includes 50 and 100 hour servicing.

BANKS IN BOTSWANA

Three banking companies operate in Botswana: Barclays, Standard Chartered and the Bank of Credit and Commerce. The last named is a relative newcomer and is established only in the capital, in Francistown, Lobatse and Kanye, where it conducts all transactions and keeps the same hours as other banks.

Barclays and Standard offer facilities in all the major towns in Botswana. Barclays' opening times, in Gaborone, Francistown and Lobatse, are:

Days	Hours
Monday to Friday (except Wednesday)	9.00 am to 2.30 pm
Wednesdays	8.15 am to 12.00 noon
Saturdays	8.15 am to 10.45 am

All other Barclays branches and all Standard Bank branches follow the following opening times:

Monday to Friday	8.15 am to 12.45 pm
Saturday	8.15 am to 10.45 am

Banks are not open on public holidays.

Both banks operate a large number of agencies around the country. The agencies do not always follow standard opening hours, opening for short periods only on certain days. Opening times can be ascertained on enquiry.

Such agencies all maintain current and savings accounts and should cash traveller's cheques. They will not deal in foreign currencies, except for the changing of Rands and Pula. Except by special arrangement, they will not be able to issue foreign exchange or traveller's cheques.

DIPLOMATIC REPRESENTATIVES RESIDENT IN BOTSWANA

ANGOLA
   Angolan Embassy. P/Bag 111, Gaborone. Tel 352599.
BRITAIN
   British High Commission. Queen's Road, Private Bag 0023, Gaborone. Tel 352841.
CANADA
   Canadian High Commission. P/Bag 00245, Gaborone. Tel 314377.

CHINA
>Embassy of the People's Republic of China. 3097 North Ring Road, P O Box 1031, Gaborone. Tel 352209.

GERMANY
>Embassy of the Federal Republic of Germany. 2nd Floor, IGI House, P O Box 315, Gaborone. Tel 353143. Telex BD 2225.

LIBYA
>The People's Bureau of the Socialist People's Libyan Arab Jamahiriya. 5508 Nyerere Drive, P O Box 180, Gaborone. Tel 352841/2. Telex BD 2501.

NIGERIA
>High Commission of the Federal Republic of Nigeria. Nigeria House, P O Box 274, Gaborone. Tel 33561-64. Telex 2415 BD.

POLAND
>Embassy of the Polish People's Republic. P/Bag 00209, Gaborone. Tel 252501.

SWEDEN
>Royal Swedish Embassy. Development House, Private Bag 0017, Gaborone. Tel 353912/3/4. Telex 2421 BD.

UNION OF SOVIET SOCIALIST REPUBLICS
>Embassy of the USSR. P O Box 81, 4711 Tawana Close, Gaborone. Tel 353389 & 353739. Telex 2595 BD.

UNITED STATES OF AMERICA
>Embassy of the United States of America. P O Box 90, Gaborone. Tel 353982/3/4. Telex 2554 BD. Fax 356947.

ZAMBIA
>High Commission of the Republic of Zambia. P O Box 362, Gaborone. Tel 351951. Telex 2416 BD.

ZIMBABWE
>High Commission of the Republic of Zimbabwe. P O Box 1232, Gaborone. Tel 353742/372202.

Consular Offices and Trade Missions based in Botswana

BELGUIM
>Belgian Consulate, First Floor, Tirelo House, The Mall. Tel 352061.

DENMARK
>Royal Danish Consulate in Botswana. Tel 353770. Fax 357995. Telex 2404 BD.

NETHERLANDS
Royal Netherlands Consulate. P O Box 457, Gaborone. Tel 357335/ 351691. Telex 2748 BD.

International Organisations based in Botswana
UNDP Tel 352121-5. Fax 356093.
SADCC Tel 351863-5.
EEC Tel 314455. Fax 313626.
UNHC for Refugees Tel 356917/22.
World Food Programme Tel 352121-5.

ENTERTAINMENT

	Gaborone	Francistown	Lobatse	Maun	Selebi-Phikwe
Cinema	*	*	*		
Theatre	*	*			
Cabaret	*				
Casino	*				
Restaurant	*	*	*	*	*
Golf	*	*	*		*
Squash	*	*	*		*
Tennis	*	*	*		*
Swimming	*	*	*		*
Sailing/Boating	*	*		*	

Many of the facilities indicated above are arranged by private clubs or hotels for their members or guests and are, strictly speaking, not available to the public. However, proprietors are most approachable and usually willing to allow visitors to use the facilities, sometimes on payment of a small fee. Restaurants have not been listed in detail, mainly because of the frequent changes in ownership, name and quality that are common in this trade.

GOVERNMENT OFFICES AND HOURS

Government office hours are Monday to Friday: 7.30 am–12.30 pm, 1.45 pm to 4.30 pm.

The following is a useful list of postal addresses and telephones of a number of Government Ministries and Departments:

Ministry	Gaborone address	Telephone/s
Office of the President	P/Bag 1	355434
Agriculture	P/Bag 003	350500
Commerce & Industry	P/Bag 004	353881-4
Finance & Development	P/Bag 008	350100
Health	P/Bag 0038	352000
Home Affairs	P/Bag 002	355212
Local Govt. & Lands	P/Bag 006	352091
Director of Vet. Services	P/Bag 0032	372769
Dept Wildlife & National Parks	P O Box 131	371405
Registrar of Companies	P O Box 102	353881
Central Statistics Office	P/Bag 0024	352200
National Archives	P/Bag 002	355525
National Museum and Art Gallery	P/Bag 0014	374616
Dept of Immigration	P O Box 942	374545
Dept of Surveys & Lands	P/Bag 0037	353251
Police Headquarters	P/Bag 0012	351161
Philatelic Bureau	P O Box 100	353304
Dept of Civil Aviation	P O Box 250	371397
Dept Customs & Excise	P/Bag 0041	312455
Central Arms Registry	P/Bag 0012	351161
Tourism Department	P/Bag 004	353024

LANGUAGE AND CUSTOMS

As you enter Botswana via the Tlokweng border gate there is a sign saying 'We hope that you will enjoy your stay here and that you will find our officials courteous. Your co-operation will help them to be even more so.'

How can one best co-operate?

Obviously every language and culture has its own norms and customs of behaviour. Politeness in one society may be the height of rudeness in another. A good place to start is with *simple courtesy and respect* for the person with whom you are dealing. Using a few phrases of the local language can also help to smooth the flow of communication.

A number of different languages are spoken in Botswana but as Setswana is the official language, greetings in this language will be understood throughout the country.

A basic lesson in Setswana will help you unravel the difference between Botswana, Batswana, Motswana and Setswana. The root 'tswana' takes on various meanings when different prefixes are added to it. So – *Botswana* is the country; *Motswana* means one of the people of the country; *Batswana* is the plural, meaning more than one person of the country; *Setswana* is the language of the country.

The Batswana set great store by politeness and courteous greeting. You don't have to be a great linguist to take your first step. In fact it must be one of the easiest languages in which to be polite. Go back to what was likely to be the very first word that you ever uttered – Ma. Lengthen the m sound as though you were about to start humming. Say 'Mma' and you have learnt the courteous form of addressing women in Botswana.

Adding 'Mma' onto a communication in English immediately makes it sound so much more polite – 'How much is this basket, Mma?'

The courteous form of addressing men is 'Rra'. The same principle applies, ie lengthen the r sound – 'Rra'.

The equivalent of 'Hello' in Setswana is 'Dumela', the stress being placed on the middle syllable. Marry your new word with the appropriate form of address and you have made a very useful investment in communicating with the people you will meet.

If you have no further linguistic ambitions the only other word to learn is, 'Go siame', which is a general all purpose end to a conversation that means 'It's all right'.

PETROL AND DIESEL

Petrol and diesel are available widely throughout the country. Prices frequently change and there is a price variation across the country. In general terms, the more remote the supply, the more expensive it will be. The greatest range is about 15 per cent above the lowest (Gaborone) price. Petrol and diesel are approximately the same price.

Fuel is available at an increasing number of outlets, on a 24-hour basis in Gaborone, Francistown and Mahalapye.

At all other centres fuel sales tend to be limited to approximately 7 am to 6 pm. However, it is generally true that the more remote the area the more amenable the owner will be to negotiation on this point.

In a previous edition, we listed all points at which fuel was sold but the list has now become somewhat unwieldy.

Instead we list all the more remote places, all of which generally sell from 7 am to 6 pm. Some close for lunch and some close on Saturday afternoons and Sundays. The places are:

Artesia, Bobonong, Bokspits, Good Hope, Hibron, Hukuntsi, Kang, Kasane, Kazangula, Letlhakane, Machaneng, Madinare, Mamashia, Metlojane, Mookane, Mopipi, Moshaneng, Moshupa, Nata, Orapa, Pitsane, Ramatlabama, Ramokwebana, Sekoma, Sefhope, Shashi, Shoshong, Sikwane, Thamaka, Tonota, Tsetsebjwe, Tshesebe, Tutume.

PROFESSIONAL SERVICES

Gaborone

Mullan & Associates.
Box 1966. Tel 314345. Tel & Fax 352878. Telex 2631 BD.
Training programmes, work and residence permit applications, personnel recruitment, selection and placement.

Whenwe Services.
Box 413. Tel 352370. Fax 372095. Telex 2299 BD.
Wide range of professional secretarial services.
(At Cresta Lodge) Tel 359292. Fax 359293.

Jasmine Secretarial Services.
Box 1051. Tel 352729.

Lobatse

Churchill Office Agencies.
Box 55. Tel 330636. Fax 330109.
Secretarial, Insurance and Agents.

Francistown

Any Other Business.
Box 610. Tel 213967. Fax 214178.
Professional secretarial services.

Maun

Maun Office Services.
Box 448. Tel 660222. Tel & Fax 660205. Telex 2482 BD.
Professional secretarial, typing, also photocopying, telex services and radio contact with most safari camps.

Merlin Services.
P/Bag 13. Tel 660351. Fax 660571. Telex 2612 BD.
Professional secretarial, typing, photocopying, telex services and radio contact with most safari camps.

Travel Wild.
P O Box 236, Maun. Tel & Fax 660493. Telex 2487 BD.
Professional secretarial, booking agency, photocopying, usual office support services and radio contact with most safari camps.

Kasane

Kasane Enterprises.
P O Box 55, Tel 250234. Fax 250223. Telex 2763 BD.
Secretarial, curios, travel agency, telex and radio contact with most safari operators.

Selebi-Phikwe

Office Services Botswana.
P/Bag 031. Tel 810910. Fax 810090. Telex 2508 BD.
Bookkeeping, company secretarial and administration services.

M & M Secretarial.
P O Box 379, Tel 810626. Fax 810364. Telex 2244 BD.
Secretarial, bookkeeping and administration.

PUBLIC HOLIDAYS

New Year's Day – 1st January
Public Holiday – 2nd January
Good Friday (see schedule below)
Public holiday on the Saturday following Good Friday
Easter Sunday
Public holiday on the Monday following Easter Sunday
Ascension Day (see schedule below)
President's Day (third Monday in July)
Public holiday on the day following President's Day
Botswana Day – 30th September
Public holiday on the day following Botswana Day
(If Botswana Day falls on a Saturday or Sunday then it will be celebrated on the following Monday.)
Christmas Day
Boxing Day

Schedule of Easter to 1995

Year	Good Friday	Ascension Day
1991	29th March	9th May
1992	17th April	28th May
1993	9th April	25th May
1994	1st April	12th May
1995	14th April	25th May

(During public holidays, all Government offices, banks, businesses and the larger shops are closed, and public transport, especially the national airline, may alter normal schedules.)

PUBLIC TRANSPORT

Air

Botswana has its own airline, Air Botswana, which provides connections between the following centres: Gaborone, Francistown, Selebi-Phikwe, Maun, Johannesburg, Lusaka and Harare. From the last three cities, all international connections can be made. There are taxis available at all airports to convey the traveller to his hotel, in the absence of any other arrangement having been made. Some hotels collect their guests.

Buses

There are reliable, regular long-distance bus services between the main towns and villages of Botswana. Numerous buses work these routes in a somewhat unscheduled manner. To make use of this service it is necessary to get to one of the signposted bus-stops on the route you wish to take – and simply wait. These facilities are far more common on the tarred roads and to villages close to the main towns. In the rural areas, on dirt roads, they exist hardly at all.

If you are starting in one of the larger urban areas you can ask for directions to the bus terminus. Most centres now have them. It is from this point that almost all the buses start their journeys and it is much easier to find one going to your destination.

Rail

The railway line from Mafikeng in Bophuthatswana to Bulawayo in Zimbabwe enters the country at Ramatlabama in the south, passes through Lobatse, Gaborone and most major towns in the east, to Francistown and Plumtree in the north.

There are two passenger services. The first is an all-class, all-stations daily train which starts in Lobatse at 4 pm every day, arriving in Plumtree the following morning. There is a reverse service from Plumtree to Lobatse.

The second service is a fast, once-a-week mail train that travels from Bulawayo to Johannesburg via Francistown, Gaborone and Mafikeng. This two-way service stops only at the main stations and has only 1st and 2nd class seats. To secure a seat in the upper classes, on either train, it is always advisable to book. For public holidays and over the busy Christmas period, extra trains are laid on.

Hitch-hiking

Conditions for the hitch-hiker in Botswana are little different from those elsewhere. On the main routes, it is more difficult to get a lift but this is compensated for by a higher volume of traffic. Often you will be asked to contribute towards petrol costs. In rural areas, there is far less traffic but drivers seem more disposed towards offering a lift.

REFERENCE MATERIAL

It has often been said that Botswana must be one of the most researched countries in Africa. Whether this is true or not, it is certainly correct to say that a great deal has been written about it.

Without a doubt, one individual whose knowledge is encyclopaedic is Alec Campbell, formerly Curator of the National Museum and Art Gallery and a resident of some twenty-five years' standing. His outstanding *Guide to Botswana* and the booklet *Sites of Historic and National Interest in and around Gaborone* are highly recommended.

Other recommended titles are:
Okavango by Johnson and Bannister
The Bushmen by Johnson and Bannister
Chobe Elephants by Bruce Aiken
Cry of the Kalahari by Mark and Delia Owens
Lost World of the Kalahari by Laurens van der Post

Newman's Birds of Botswana by Kenneth Newman

Okavango, Jewel of the Kalahari by Karen Ross

The Swamp Book by Murray-Hudson *et al*

Okavango from the Air by Herman Potgieter and Clive Walker

Kalahari; Rivers of Sand by Degré, Roberet, Knight & Cherry

Guide to Kalahari Gemsbok National Park by Gus Mills

Newman's Birds of Southern Africa by Kenneth Newman

Roberts' Birds of Southern Africa by Gordon Maclean

Kalahari: Life's Variety in Dune and Delta by Mike Main

Any handbook of snakes and reptiles of Southern Africa, such as *Snake versus Man* by Johan Marais

Any guide to mammals of Southern Africa, such as *Land Mammals of Southern Africa* by Reay Smithers

Published by and obtainable from the Botswana Society, at the National Museum, Gaborone, are several of their outstanding works, including:

Botswana Notes and Records – the Society's annual journal.

Settlement in Botswana – proceedings of a symposium on population, history and land use planning, including problems of migration and urbanisation.

Drought in Botswana – proceedings of a symposium on the ecological consequences and strategic responses to drought, including recognition and prediction of drought conditions.

The Okavango Delta – which looks at the economy and ecology of one of the world's major wetlands.

The Management of Botswana's Environment – a look at the Government's national conservation strategy in relation to development planning.

For the serious researcher the National Archives in Gaborone is an excellent source of material and, in this regard, another Botswana Society publication, *The Bibliography of Botswana* by Karala Jones, is an indispensable source of information.

For those with a less serious interest, there are national lending libraries in all the larger towns which offer an excellent range of both non-fiction and fiction titles.

SERVICE ORGANISATIONS AND SOCIETIES

Alliance Française	Box 1817, Gaborone. Tel 351650.
American Women's International Association	Meets every second Wednesday monthly, Gaborone. Tel 357680/2/3.
Botswana Bird Club	National Museum, Gaborone. Box 71, Gaborone. Tel 351500.
Botswana Red Cross Society	Box 485, Gaborone. Tel 352465 & 312351.
The Botswana Society	National Museum, Gaborone. Box 71, Gaborone. Tel 351500.
The Women's Corona Society	Meets monthly, Gaborone, Lobatse. P O Box 820, Gaborone.
Jaycees	Meet every Monday, Gaborone Sun Hotel, 7 pm. Visitors welcome.
Kalahari Conservation Society	P O Box 859, Gaborone. Tel 314259. Fax 374557. Occasional lectures as advertised.
Lions	Zones 13 and 14, region 5, District 412. Clubs at Boteti (Orapa/Lethlakane) P/Bag 4, Lethlakane; Gaborone, Box 618; Francistown, Box 412; Lobatse, Box 118; Palapye, P/Bag 7; S/Phikwe, Box 59. Gaborone Club meets at 7.30 pm on the 2nd and 4th Thursday of each month and has a bookstall in the Mall each Saturday morning. Additional information can be acquired by writing to club Secretaries. Guest Lions welcome.
Rotary	Gaborone, meets every Friday except public holidays, 12.30 pm, Gaborone Sun Hotel. P O Box 1010, Gaborone. Selebi-Phikwe, meets every Tuesday, 7.30 pm, Bosele Hotel. P O Box 675, Selebi-Phikwe.
Round Table	Branches in Francistown, Jwaneng, Orapa, Selebi-Phikwe, Lobatse and Gaborone. Gaborone, meets 2nd and 4th Thursday. Various venues, evenings. P O Box 372, Gaborone.
Ladies' Circle	P O Box 20646, Bontleng, Gaborone. Monthly meetings.
Photographic Society	Meets 2nd Wednesday, monthly, Gaborone Sun Hotel, 8 pm.

SHOPPING

In general terms, it is true to say that in the larger centres most day-to-day consumer items are readily available. On the other hand, there are very few, if any, really top quality shops such as one might find in a modern shopping complex elsewhere. The supply is more concerned with function than luxury.

There are good supermarkets in Lobatse, Gaborone, Mahalapye, Selebi-Phikwe, Francistown and Maun. In these towns you will also find good clothing stores, bottle-stores, hardware shops, chemists, bookshops and curio shops. In the larger centres imported fresh vegetables can usually be purchased without difficulty. Mondays and days following public holidays may sometimes present the shopper with unexpected, temporary shortages, particularly of fresh products such as milk and vegetables.

Hours of trading are generally from 8 am until 5 pm, although bottle-stores open at 10 am and close at 7 pm. Some shops close for an hour at lunchtime. Again, in most of the larger centres there is at least one establishment which remains open until as late as 8 or 9 pm, selling the usual range of essential household requirements. It is usually this type of general dealer to which one can turn on public holidays, for they often remain open during these periods as well. During such holidays, all Government offices, businesses, banks and the larger shops are closed.

Botswana does not have a sophisticated photographic market; if you are using specialist film, it is best to bring it with you. Colour slide film is only available in the main centres, and in some of the safari camps. There is a small danger that it might be out of date or ill-protected against the heat and thus damaged. Some centres can process several types of colour prints on the 'one hour' processing machines which are becoming common, but all colour slides and prints that do not fit these machines are sent for processing outside the country.

In the small villages around the country, shopping is a very much more precarious activity. Almost every village has its store or stores – and a surprising number of them have bottle-stores. The range of goods available in these outlets is sometimes amazing. We have, for example, purchased imported French wine in the most astonishing places! Generally, household basics will certainly be available – sugar, dried milk, tea, some kind of coffee, cigarettes, soap and soap powders, tinned fruit, corned beef, etc. The bottle-stores usually restrict themselves to soft drinks, beer and the cheaper spirits – but they are quite capable, occasionally, of unearthing an unexpected bottle of wine or a good whisky! Very few stores have refrigerators so you will get nothing cold and nothing fresh.

Increasingly in the more popular tourist areas, roadside vendors of curios, ranging from woven baskets to carved wooden objects, are becoming more common. The standard of workmanship varies from excellent to poor, so shop carefully. There are no fixed prices – each transaction must be negotiated.

TELEPHONE SYSTEM

Broadly speaking, all the larger towns have automatic telephone exchanges, all of which are currently being modernised and improved.

Those towns are: Francistown, Gaborone, Jwaneng, Kanye, Kasane, Lobatse, Mahalapye, Maun, Mochudi, Molepolole, Nata, Orapa, Palapye, Ramotswa, Selebi-Phikwe and Serowe.

All the above are interconnected on an internal trunk-dialling system and there is international direct dialling.

The following rural areas also have telephone systems, operated by manual exchanges for limited hours, generally from 8 am until 5 pm during the week and from 8 am until midday on Saturday. Both national and international calls can be made with the assistance of the operator. These towns and villages are: Bobonong, Ghanzi, Lentsweletau, Lerala, Letlhakane, Letlhakeng, Machaneng, Makaleng, Mankgodi, Manyana, Mathangwane, Matsiloje, Mmadinare, Moeng, Moshupa, Oodi, Ootse, Pilikwe, Pitsane, Ramokwebana, Sebina, Sedibeng, Sefhare, Sefhophe, Serule, Shashe, Sherwood, Shoshong, Sikwane, Thamaga, Tonata, Tshesebe and Tutume.

In areas where there are no telephones, emergency messages can be passed by two means. The police will accept messages, including international telegrams. Most of the professional hunters and safari operators operate a radio network, through which messages can be passed.

Telex services
There are public telex and fax services at the post offices of the following centres: Francistown, Gaborone, Ghanzi, Kanye, Lobatse, Maun and Selebi-Phikwe.

Miscellaneous information 165

TRAVEL AGENCIES

Maun

Air Botswana	P O Box 191, Maun. Tel 60391. Telex 2492 BD.
Bonaventures	P O Box 201, Maun. Tel 660502/3. Telex 2616 BD.
Merlin Services & Travel	P/Bag 13, Maun. Tel 660351. Fax 660571. Telex 2612 BD.
Okavango Tours & Safaris	P O Box 39, Maun. Tel 660220/660339. Fax 660589. Telex 2484 BD.
Travel Wild	P O Box 236, Maun. Tel and Fax 260493. Telex 2487 BD.

Francistown

Air Botswana	P O Box 222, Francistown. Tel 212393/4. Telex 2213 BD.
Phuti Travel	P O Box 82, Francistown. Tel 213909. Telex 2460 BD.
Travel Services Botswana	P O Box 401, Francistown. Tel 212033. Fax 212828. Telex 2949 BD.

Gaborone

Air Botswana	P O Box 92, Gaborone. Tel 352812/351921. Fax 374802. Telex 2413 BD.
Manica Travel	P O Box 1188, Gaborone. Tel 352021. Fax 352021. Telex 2523 BD.
Kudu Travel	P O Box 1241, Gaborone. Tel 372224. Fax 374224. Telex 2470 BD.
Phuti Travel & Tours	P/Bag 00297, Gaborone. Tel 314166. Fax 374290. Telex 2521 BD.
Travel Services South	P/Bag 00282, Gaborone. Tel 374740. Fax 356111.

166 Botswana

Tswana Travel & Tours	P O Box 1509, Gaborone. Tel 357047.
Kasane	
Kasane Enterprises	P O Box 55, Kasane. Tel 250234. Fax 250223.
Lobatse	
Air Botswana	P O Box 392, Lobatse. Tel 330502/330501. Telex 2290 BD.
Selebi-Phikwe	
Air Botswana	P O Box 2, Selebi-Phikwe. Tel 810654/810780. Telex 2248 BD.
Phuti Travel	P O Box 323, Selebi-Phikwe. Tel 810914. Fax 810781. Telex 2285 BD.
Travel Bags	P O Box 556, Selebi-Phikwe. Tel 814106. Fax 814107.

VEHICLE HIRE

Gaborone

Avis Rent A Car	Sir Seretse Khama Airport. P O Box 790, Gaborone. Tel 313039. Fax 312205. Telex 2723 BD.
Van & Truck Hire	(vans, trucks and 4 × 4's). Plot 5649, Nakedi Road, Broadhurst. P O Box 916, Gaborone. Tel & Fax 312280.
Bushlink	4 × 4s, fully equipped for camping. P/Bag 00314, Gaborone. Tel 371480. Fax 371480
Economic Car Hire	P O Box 1966, Gaborone. Tel 314345. Fax 352878.
Holiday Car Rentals	P/Bag 0016, Gaborone. Tel 351111, 353970 (airport). Fax 312280.

Francistown

Avis	Francistown Airport. P O Box 222, Francistown. Tel 213901. Fax 212867. Telex 2723 BD.

Miscellaneous information 167

Holiday Car Rentals Francistown Airport. P O Box 717, Francistown. Tel 214524. Fax 214526.

Maun

Avis Safari Hire Maun Airport. P O Box 130, Maun. Tel 660258. Fax 660258. Telex 2803 BD.

Holiday Car Rentals Opposite airport. P/Bag 13, Maun. Tel 660351. Fax 660571. Telex 2612 BD.

Island Safari Lodge (4 × 4 vehicles) P O Box 116, Maun. Tel 660300. Telex 2482 BD.

Travel Wild (4 × 4 & LDVs restricted to Maun area only) P O Box 236, Maun. Tel 660493. Telex 2487 BD.

Kasane

Bushlink (4 × 4s, fully equipped for camping) P O Box 55, Kasane. Tel 250234. Fax 250223.

Holiday Car Rentals P O Box 197, Kasane. Tel 250226. Fax 250223. Telex 2763 BD.

MAPS OF TOWNS

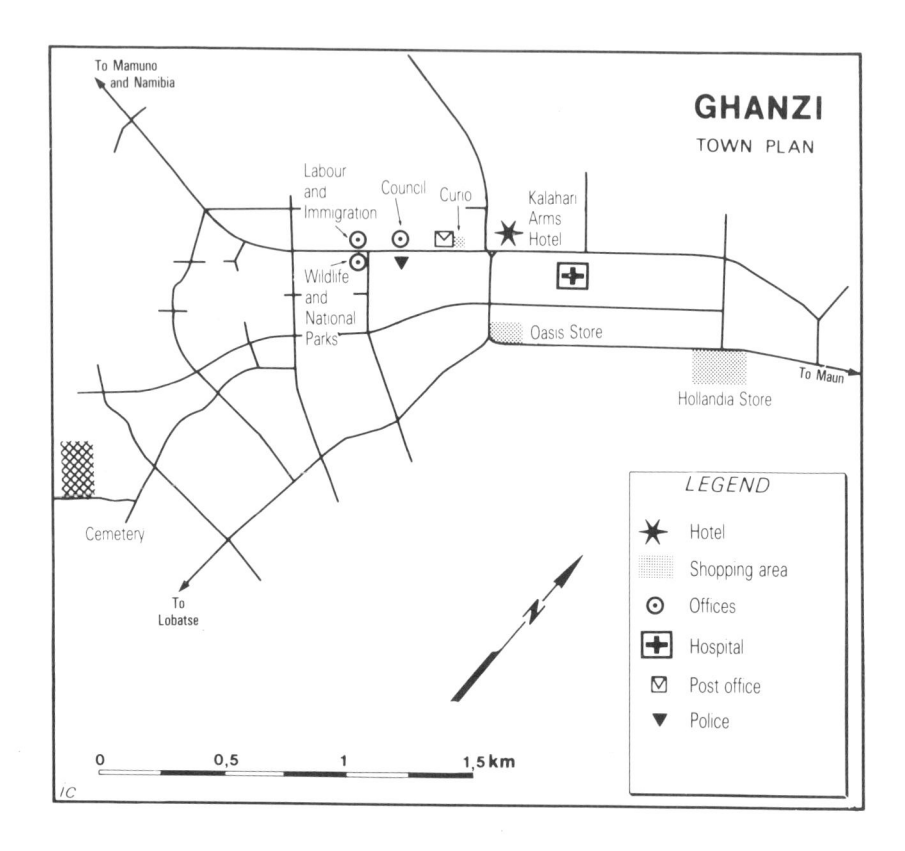

Miscellaneous information 169

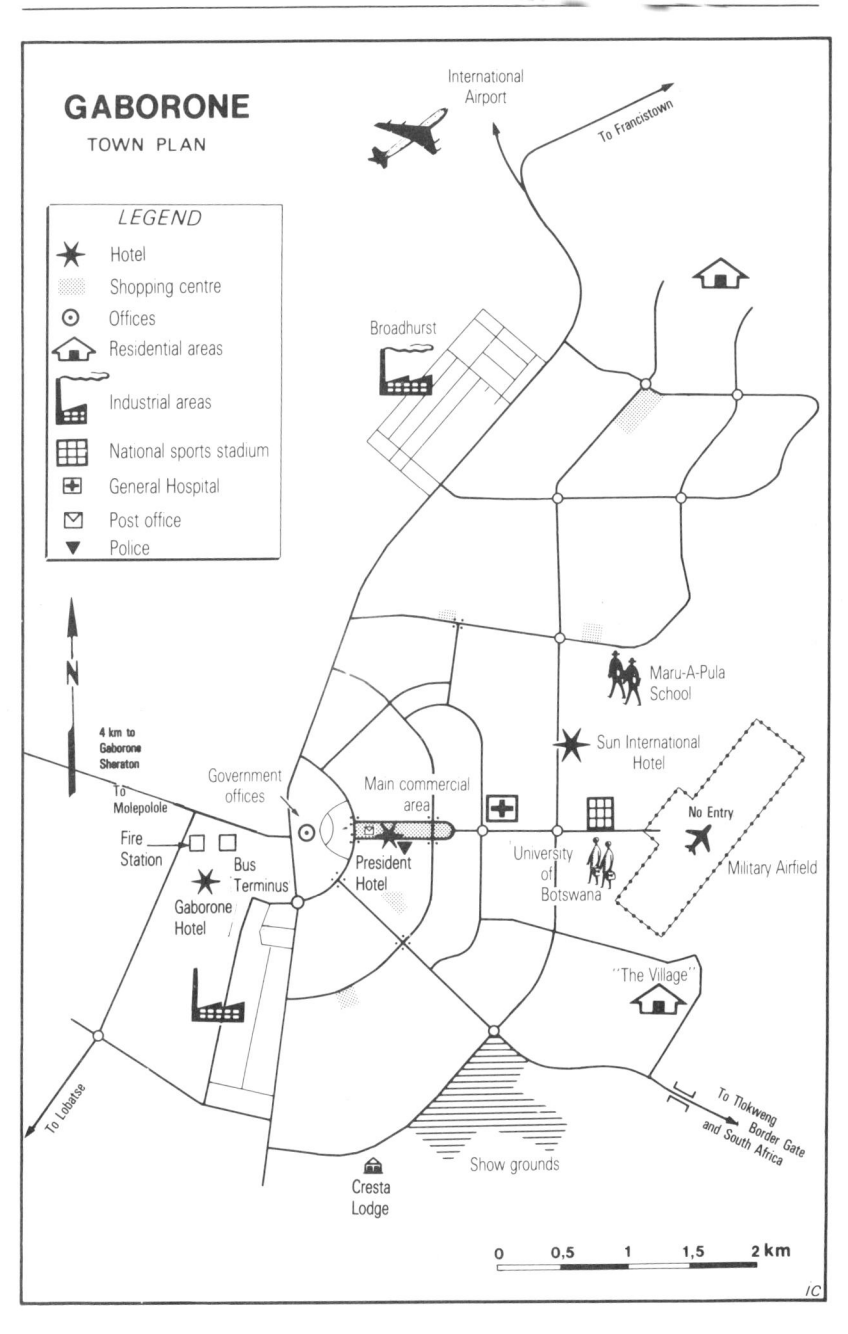

GABORONE
TOWN PLAN

LEGEND
- ★ Hotel
- ▒ Shopping centre
- ⊙ Offices
- 🏠 Residential areas
- 🏭 Industrial areas
- ⊞ National sports stadium
- ✚ General Hospital
- ✉ Post office
- ▼ Police

International Airport
To Francistown
Broadhurst
4 km to Gaborone Sheraton
To Molepolole
Fire Station
Bus Terminus
Gaborone Hotel
Government offices
Main commercial area
President Hotel
Maru-A-Pula School
Sun International Hotel
University of Botswana
No Entry
Military Airfield
"The Village"
To Tlokweng Border Gate and South Africa
Show grounds
Cresta Lodge
To Lobatse

0   0,5   1   1,5   2 km

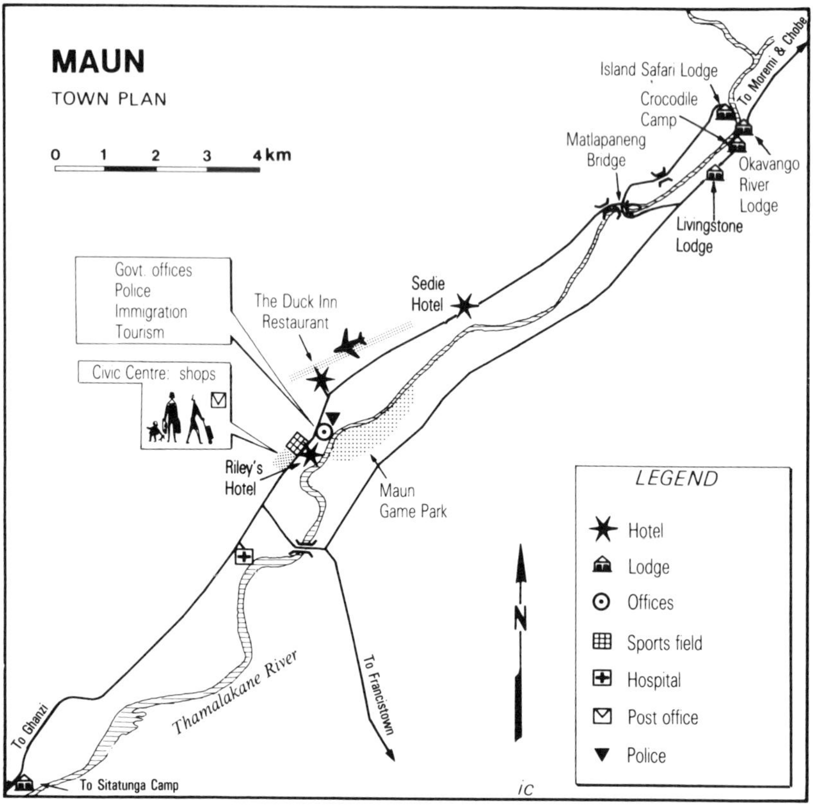
MAUN
TOWN PLAN
0 1 2 3 4km
Island Safari Lodge
Crocodile Camp
Matlapaneng Bridge
To Moremi & Chobe
Okavango River Lodge
Livingstone Lodge
Govt. offices
Police
Immigration
Tourism
Civic Centre: shops
The Duck Inn Restaurant
Sedie Hotel
Riley's Hotel
Maun Game Park
LEGEND
Hotel
Lodge
Offices
Sports field
Hospital
Post office
Police
N
Thamalakane River
To Francistown
To Ghanzi
To Sitatunga Camp
ic

Miscellaneous information 171

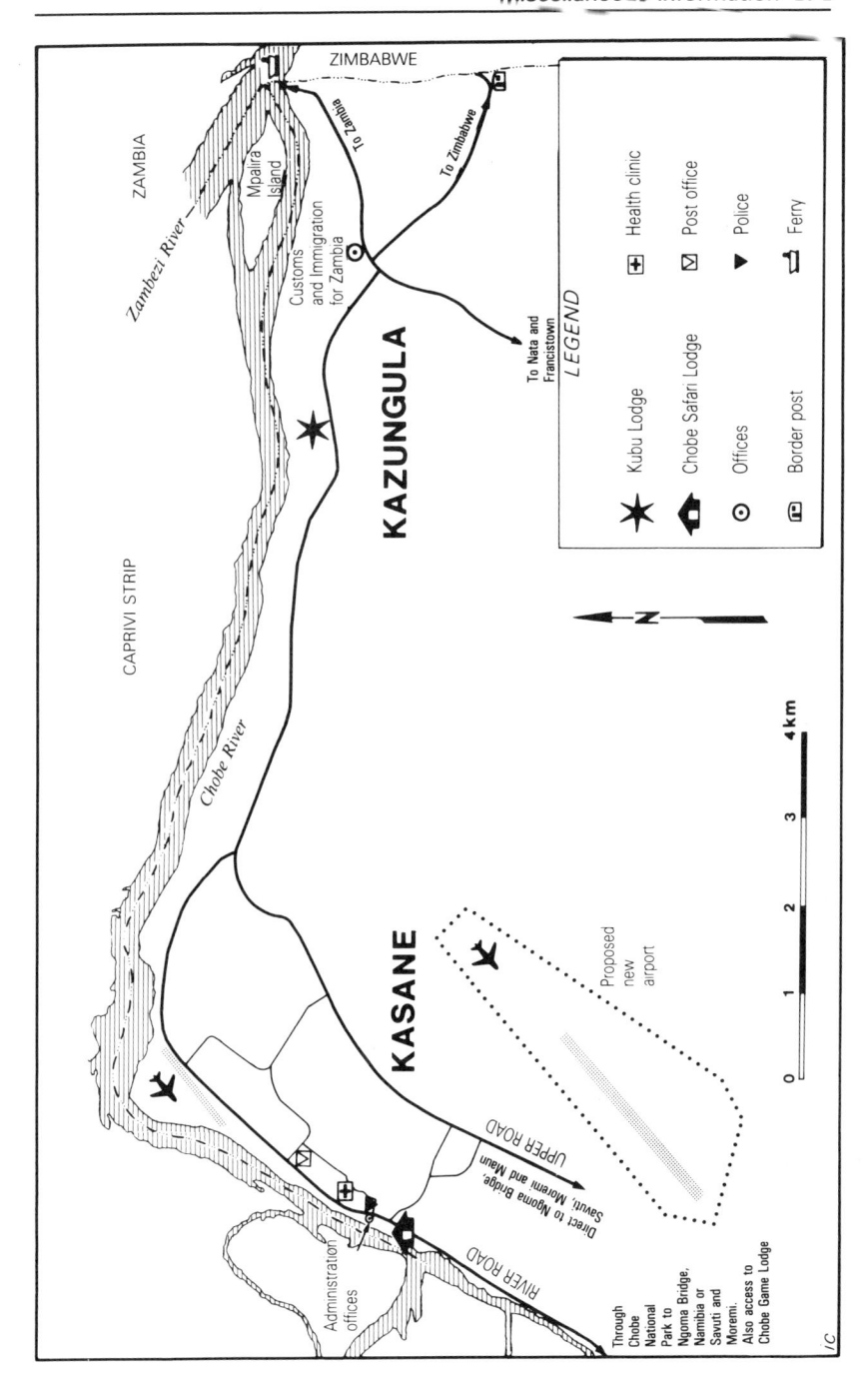

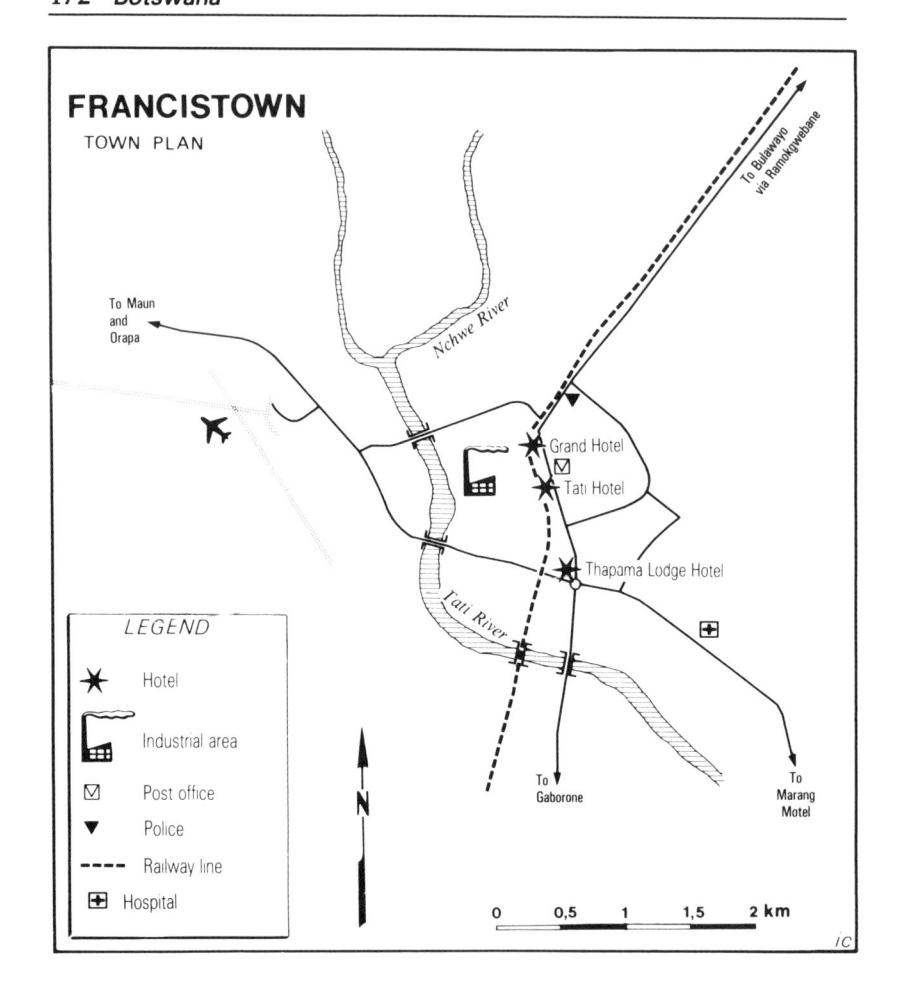

FRANCISTOWN
TOWN PLAN

Miscellaneous information 173

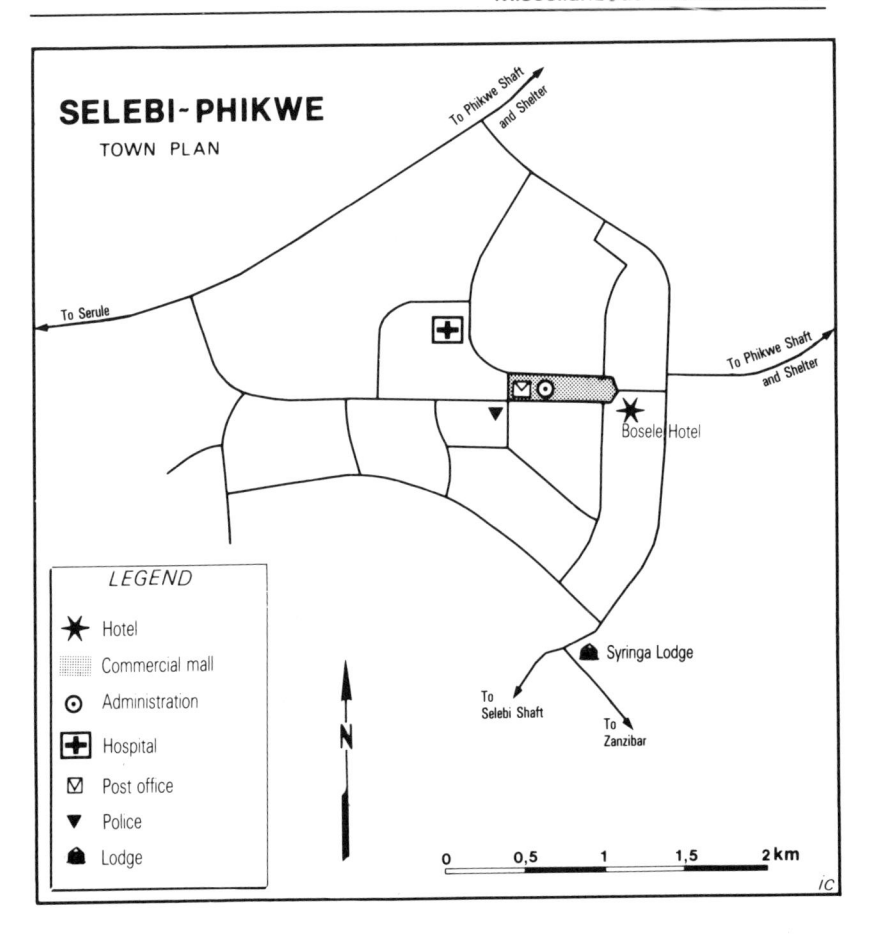

SELEBI-PHIKWE
TOWN PLAN

LEGEND
★ Hotel
▨ Commercial mall
⊙ Administration
✚ Hospital
✉ Post office
▼ Police
🛖 Lodge

LOBATSE
TOWN PLAN

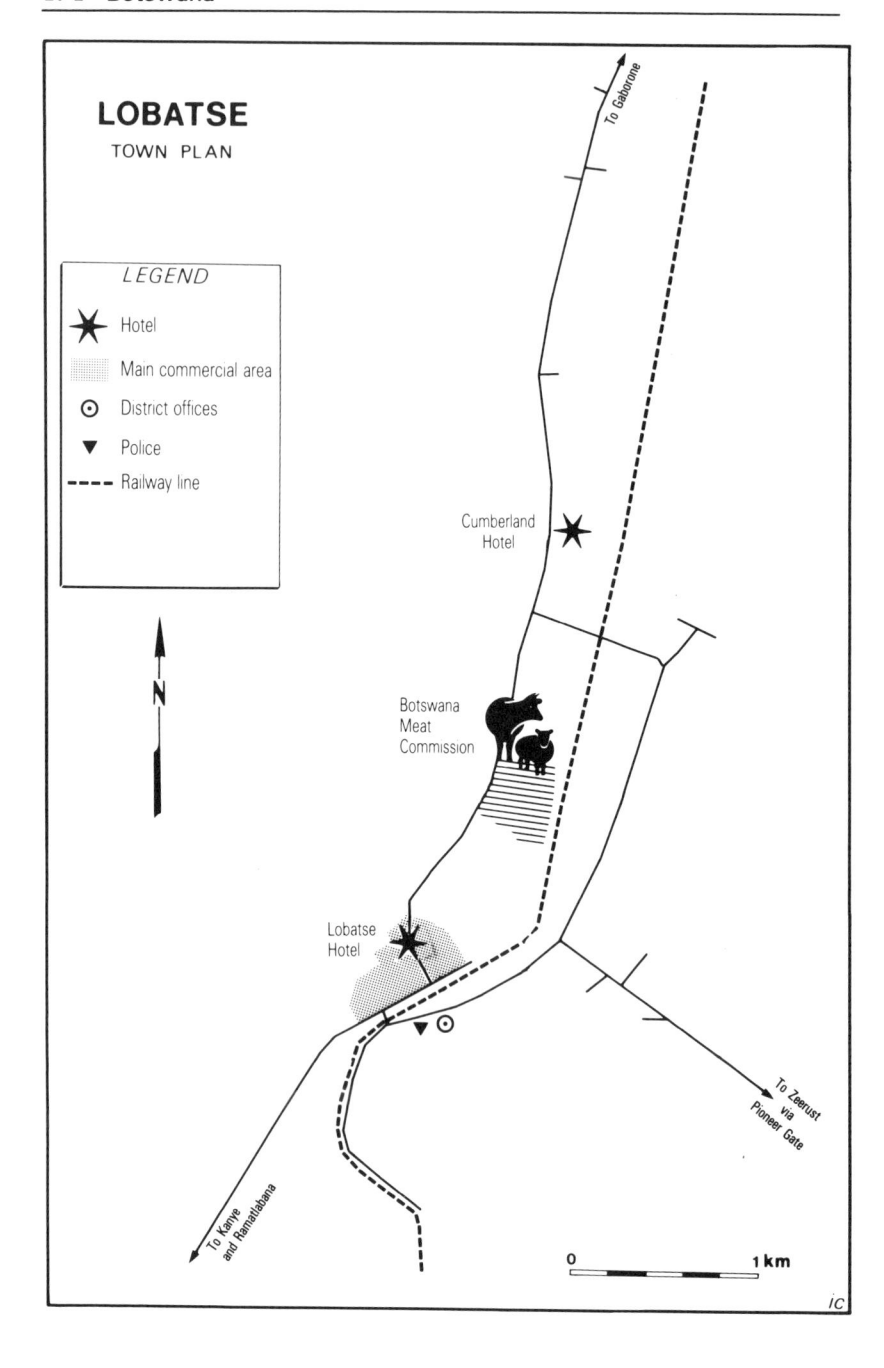

LEGEND
- ★ Hotel
- Main commercial area
- ⊙ District offices
- ▼ Police
- ---- Railway line

N

To Gaborone

Cumberland Hotel

Botswana Meat Commission

Lobatse Hotel

To Kanye and Ramatlabama

To Zeerust via Pioneer Gate

0   1 km

INDEX

Acacia woodland 25
Accidents
 road 83-4
 with livestock 83-4
Aerial photographs 72
Aha Hills 3-4
 directions 52
 sink-holes 3, 4
AIDS 67
Air Botswana 159
Aircraft
 charter 151
 maintenance 151
Airline, national 159
Airports 78
Airstrip, Tsodilo Hills 24
Alliance Francaise 162
Allowances, currency 79-80
Aloes 16
Ancient Lake; see Paleolake
Andara 29
Anthropological research 4
Aoub River 9

Baines, Thomas 16, 17
Baines' Baobabs 16-17, 48-9, 93
Bakalahari Schwelle 11
Banking hours 152
Banks 152
Baobabs 14, 15, 16-17, 39
 Baines' 16-17, 48-9, 93
 Chapman's 15, 39
 Green's 15, 39
Barnard, Izak 25, 147
Behaviour in the bush 85-8
Bilharzia 67-8
Bird Club, Botswana 62, 162
Birdlife 61-2
Bites, snake 69
Bohelabatho Pan 36
Bohelabatwana Pan 36
Bokspits 4, 8, 9

Border posts 77
Boteti River 12, 13, 14, 93
Botswana Bird Club 162
Botswana Notes and Records 4, 7
Botswana Society 4, 7, 162
Breakdowns, vehicle 84-5
Buses 159
Bush driving 88-92
Bushlink Safaris 149

Camera care 64-5
Camp beds 75
Camping
 equipment 74-6
 tips 86-8
Campsites
 Baines' Baobabs 93
 National Parks & Reserves 142-6
 selection 87
Campsites, public
 Central Kalahari 94
 Chobe 93, 143-4
 Kalahari Gemsbok 94
 Khutse 94
 Makgadikgadi 93, 145
 Moremi 93, 144-5
 Nxai Pan 93, 145
Caprivi route 29
Caprivi Strip 29-30
Cats, permits for 80
Cattle, numbers at Lake Ngami 11
Central Kalahari Game Reserve 5, 6, 9, 59, 94
Chapman's Baobab 15, 39
Charter, aircraft 151
Children on safari 60
Chloroquin tablets 65, 67
Chobe National Park 5, 58, 93
Chobe River, fishing 62-3
Climate 57
Climatic change 6, 15, 19
Clinics 70

176 Botswana

Clothing 65, 66, 76
Clutch and brake fluid 85
Compass 65
Consular offices 152-4
Cooking utensils 75-6
Cooper, Simon 23
Courtesy 155-6
Crocodile 88
Cry of the Kalahari 5
Currency allowances 79-80
Customs, local 155-6
Customs 77-81
  airports 78
  boats 79
  border posts 77
  currency allowances 79-80
  health certificates 80
  length of stay 81
  visa requirements 80
  visitor requirements 78-81

Deception Valley 5
Diarrhoea 70
Diesel 156-7
Diplomatic representatives 152-4
Distance chart 56
Dobe 3, 4
Dogs, permits for 80
Dorsland Trekkers 8
Drink 73
Driver's licences 81
Driving
  accidents 83-4
  bush 88-92
  gravel roads 91
  night 83, 92
  road hazards 82
  safety belts 82
  speed limits 82
  tarmac roads 82-4
  water 91
  wild animals 86
Drotsky's Cave 3, 4, 5-6
  directions 51
  photography 7
Dunes *see* Sand dunes
Dust 70

Eaton, Dick 8
Elephant safaris 146
Embassies 152-4
Emergencies, vehicle; *see* Vehicle
  breakdowns
Entertainment 154
Entry fees, National Parks 95-7
Equipment and vehicle hire 149

Facilities, National Parks 93-4
Fees, entry, National Parks 95-7
Fences; *see* Veterinary fences
Firearms 79
First aid 70
Fishing 62-3
Flat batteries 85
Food 73
Footwear 66
Fuel, vehicles 156-7

Gabasadi Island 15-16, 39
Gaborone Game Reserve 95
Game Reserves
  Central Kalahari 5, 6, 9, 59
  Gaborone 95
  Khutse 60
  Mabuasehube 11-12, 60
  Makgadikgadi 12-13, 59
  Mannyelanong 60
  Mhlango 29
  Moremi 13-14, 58
Game, feeding of 86
Gas cooking 75
Gears, use of 89
Ghanzi 7-8
Government hours 154-5
Government offices 154-5
Grass seeds, radiators 90-1
Grasslands 12-13
Green, Frederick Joseph 14
Green's Baobab; *see* Green's Tree
Green's Tree 14-15, 39
Gubatsaa Hills 19
Guns 79
Gweta village 14

Haacke, Wolf 69
Hambukushu people 24

Index 177

Health
 certificates 80
 precautions 66–71
Herero people 11
Hills, Tsodilo 23–5
Hire
 equipment 149
 vehicles 149, 166–7
Hitch-hiking 160
HIV virus 67
Holidays, public 158–9
Hospitals 70
Hotels
 in towns 97–9
 see also Lodges
Hottentot people 23
Hours, government 154–5
Hukuntsi 23
Hunting blinds 16

Initials, carved in trees 14, 15
Insurance, motor vehicle 81
Islands
 Ntwetwe Pan 15
 Sowa Pan 20–2
Islands, land of a thousand 15
Islands of vegetation 12
Izak Barnard 25, 147

Jacking up a vehicle 84

Kalahari Conservation Society 95, 162
Kalahari Gemsbok National Park 8, 60, 94
Kalahari sand, depth 17
Karakul industry 4
Katima Mulilo 29
Kgama-Kgama Pan 16
Khakhea 12
Khutse Game Reserve 9–10, 60, 94
Kilometre chart 56
Kokoro Island 22
Kubu Island 14, 21
 directions to 44–5
Kudiakam Pan 17
Kukonje Island 22
Kuruman River 35
Kwakai Pan 36

Kwihabe Hills 3
Kwihabe River 6
Lake Ngami; see Ngami
Lake River 17
Language 155–6
Laurens van der Post 23
Lehututu 23
Length of stay 81
Licences, driver's 81
Limpopo River 19
 fishing 62
Lions, service club 162
Livestock, in accidents 83–4
Livingstone, David
 at Ngami 10
 crossing pans 14
Lodges
 Francistown 102–3
 Gweta 103–4
 Kasane 105–8
 listing 101–2
 Maun 109–14
 Moremi 114–26
 Nata 131–2
 Savuti 126–31
 Tuli 132–7
 Western Delta 137–42
 see also hotels
Lokgwabe 23
Lost World of the Kalahari 23

Mababe Depression 19–20
Mabuasehube Game Reserve 11, 12, 60, 93–4
Magwikhwe Sand Ridge 19, 54
Maintenance, aircraft 151
Makgadikgadi Game Reserve 12–13, 93
 Njuca Hills 12–13, 47
 when to visit 59
 Xhumaga Camp Site 12–13
Makgadikgadi grasslands 12–13
Makgadikgadi pans 14–15, 20–3
 birdlife 61–2
Makoba Fence 37
Makolwane a ga Wateka 15
Malaria 65, 66–7
Mamuno 25

178 Botswana

Mannyelanong Game Reserve 60, 94
Maps 71, 72
Francistown 172
Gaborone 169
Ghanzi 168
Kasane 171
Kazungula 171
Lobatse 174
Makgadikgadi 40
Maun 170
Selebi-Phikwe 173
Marais, Johan 69
Masetlheng Pan 25, 36
Mata Mata 9
Mekoro 14, 18
Mgobe wa Takhu, waterhole 15
Mhlango Game Reserve 29
Mileage chart 56
Mirages 12
Mobile safari operators 146–50
  factors affecting price 149–50
  list of 147–9
  starting points 146–7
Mohembo Gate 17, 29
Mokoro 14, 18
Molopo River 34
Mopipi 38
Mopipi Reservoir 38
Moremi Game Reserve 13–14, 58, 93
Mosu 22
Museum, Transvaal 69

Nata River Delta 22
National airline 159
National Parks 58–60, 93–4
  Chobe 5, 58
  entry fees 95–7
  facilities in 93–4
  Kalahari Gemsbok 8, 60
  Nxai Pan 16–17, 59
Ncojane Farms 25
Ngami, Lake 10–11, 50–1
  birdlife 61
Ngoma Bridge 29
Ngotwane River 95
Ngwaatle Pan 36
Ngwezumba Dam 55

Njuca Hills 15, 12–13, 47
Nossob Camp 9
Nossob River 9
Ntwetwe Pan 14–16
  Gabasadi Island 15–16
  HRH Prince Charles 16
  hunting blinds 16
  islands 15
Nxai Pan National Park 16–17, 59, 93

Okavango Delta 13–14, 17–18, 58–9
  annual flood 17
  fishing 62–3
  tectonics 10–11
  vertical fall 17
  when to visit 58
Okwa River 32
Orapa Mine 14, 37
  permits 37
Otse 94
Owens, Mark and Delia 5

Packing
  clothing 76
  equipment 75
  vehicle 72
Paleolake 15, 20–1, 32
  bed 15
  origins 19
  sand ridge 19, 54
  shoreline 15, 19, 54
Palm trees 15
Pans
  Bohelabatho 36
  Bohelobatwana 36
  description 11
  Kgama-Khama 16
  Kudiakam 16
  Kwakai 36
  largest 25
  Mabuasehube 11–12
  Makgadikgadi 14–16, 20–3
  Masetlheng 25, 36
  Ngwaatle 36
  Rappel's 4
  shape 11
  Tshane 23
  Ukwi 25

Index

vehicles 84
Zonye 36
Parssarge, S 11
Permits
  boats 79
  firearms 79
  pets 80
Petrol 156-7
Pets, permits for 80
Photographs, aerial 72
Photography 64-5
Drotsky's Cave 7
Poppa Falls 29
Prince Charles, HRH 16
Professional services 157-8
Public holidays 158-9
Pyramids 43

Rabies 68
Radiators, grass seeds 90-1
Rail transport 160
Rainy season 57
Rappel's Pan 4
Reading, Botswana 160-1
Red Cross Society 162
Reference material 160-1
Research, anthropological 4
Rhodes Trekkers 8
Rifles 79
Rift Valley 17
Rivers
  Boteti 12, 13, 14, 17
  Kuruman 35
  Lake 17
  Limpopo 19
  Molopo 34
  Ngotwane 95
  Okwa 32
  Thamalakane 17
  Thaoge 10
  Upper Zambezi 19
Road tax, vehicles 79
Roads
  changeability 26
  gravel 91
  tarmac 82
Rotary 162

Round Table 162
Route
Caprivi 29-30
1 Gaborone-Khutse 30
2 Gaborone-Mabuasehube 30-1
3 Gaborone-Ghanzi 31-3
4 Jwaneng-Sekoma-Khakhea-Werda 33
5 Werda-Bokspits 34
6A Hukuntsi-Masetlheng 35-6
6 Kang-Tshabong 35
7A Mopipi-Deception Valley 37-8
7B(1) Orapa-Gweta 38-9
7B(2) Western Islands 40
7B(3) Maun road to Gabasadi Island 40-4
7B(4) Kubu-Gweta 41
7 Serowe-Orapa 36-7
8(1) east Sowa 41-2
8(2) west Sowa 42-4
8(3) south Sowa 45
9 Francistown-Maun 45-6
10 Makgadikgadi Game Reserve 46-8
11 Nxai Pan and Baines' Baobabs 48-9
12 Maun-Ghanzi 49-50
13 Ghanzi-Mamuno 50
14 Maun-Lake Ngami 50-1
15 Maun-Drotsky's Cave 51
16 Drotsky's Cave-Aha Hills 52
17 Maun-Tsodilo 52-3
18 Maun-Moremi-Savuti 53-5
19 Savuti-Kasane 55
Routes
  numerical 30-55
  some common 27-8
Rubbish, removal of 87
Ruins, stone walled 21

Safari operators 18
Safari South 146-7
Safety belts 82
Salt tablets 70
Sand dunes, Tsodilo Hills 24
Sand ridges 19, 27
San 16
  Tsodilo Hills 24-5
  hunting blinds 16

180 Botswana

new villages 25
Savuti 18–20, 55
Savuti Channel 19, 20, 55
Schwelle, Bakalahari 11
Service organisations 162
Services, professional 157–8
Shakawe Fishing Camp, petrol 24
Shakwe 30
Shoes 66
Shopping 163
Shorelines 15, 19, 21
Simon Cooper 23
Sink holes, Aha Hills 3, 4
Slave and master cylinder 85
Sleeping
   in open 75
   in tents 87
Sleeping sickness 68
Snakebite 69
Sutherland method 69
Soda Ash Project 23, 42
Sowa Pan 14, 20–3
   pyramids 43
   soda ash project 23, 42
Spare parts, vehicles 71
Speed limits 82
Spotlights 92
Spring, Sowa Pan 22
Stay in Botswana, length of 81
Steering, bush driving 90
Sting, scorpion 69
Stone Age
   Late 4, 22
   Middle 4
Stone Age sites
   Ntwetwe 16
   Sowa 22
Street maps 72
Suncare 65, 70
Sutherland Method 69

Tswana people 3, 11, 13
Telephones 164
Telex 164
Temperatures 57–8
Thamalakane River 17
Thaoge River 10

Third Bridge 87, 93, 145
Ticks, dislodging 68–9
Tick-bite fever 68
Town maps; see Maps
Trains 160
Transport
   air 159
   buses 159
   rail 160
Transvaal Museum 69
Travel agencies 165
Tsabong 12
Tse-tse fly
   clothing 65
   sleeping sickness 68
Tshane 23
Tshane Pan 23
Tsodilo Hills 23–5
   airstrip 24
   directions 52–3
Twee Rivieren Camp 8, 9
Tyre pressures 90

Ukwi Pan 25
Union's End 9
Upper Zambezi River 19
Utensils, cooking 75–6

Van der Post, L 23
Van der Westhuizen, Klaas 4
Van Zyl, Hendrik 7, 8
   initials 14
Van Zyl's Cutting 8
Vehicles
   breakdowns 84–5
   choice of 27
   driver's licences 81
   fuel 156–7
   hire 166–7
   insurance 81
   packing 72
   road tax 79
   spares 71
Venom 69
Veterinary fences 37, 38, 39, 41, 45
Victoria Falls 19
Villages
   Bokspits 4, 8, 9

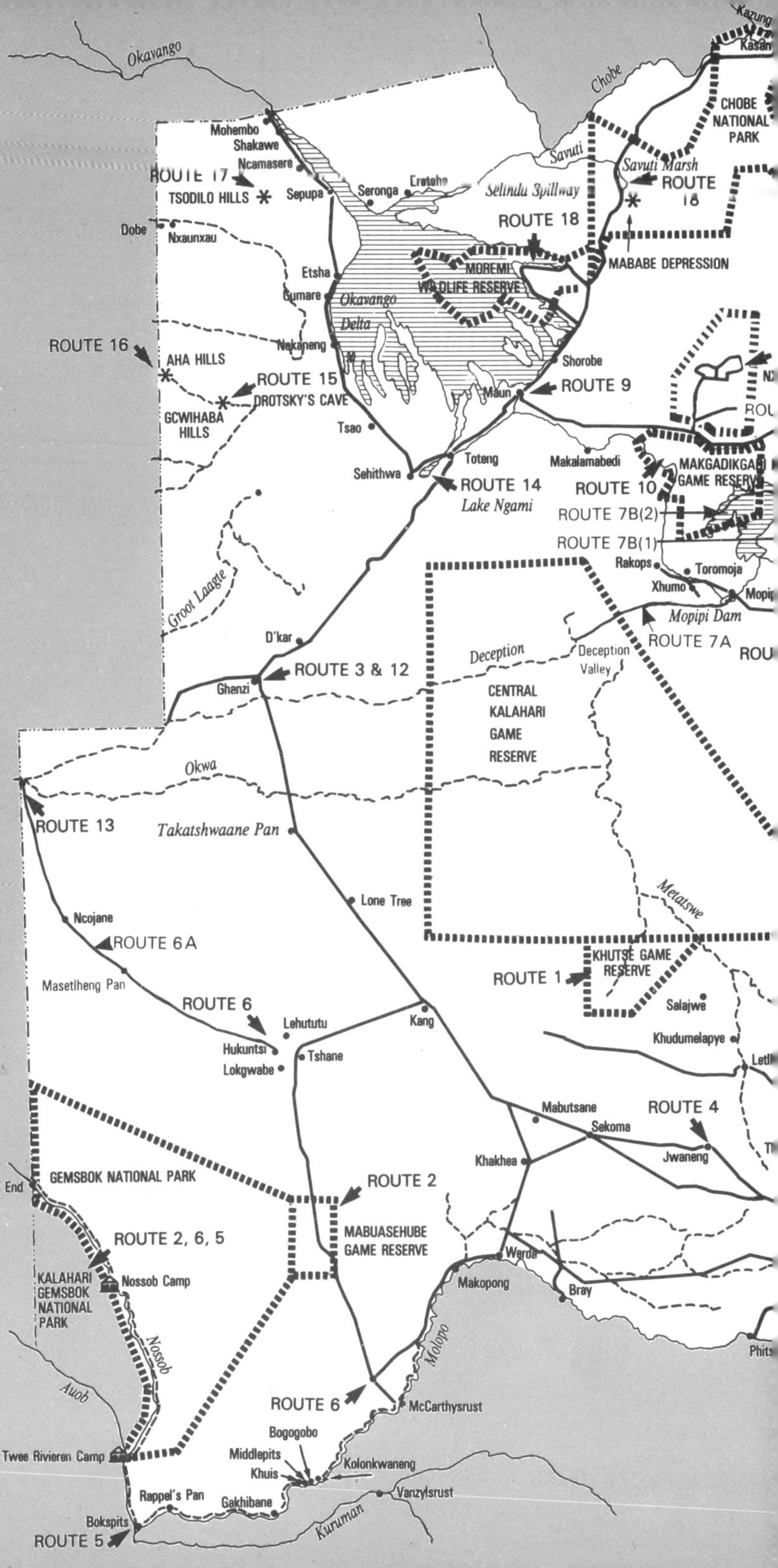

Okavango
Chobe
CHOBE NATIONAL PARK
Savuti
Savuti Marsh
ROUTE 18
Mohembo
Shakawe
Ncamasere
ROUTE 17
TSODILO HILLS
Sepupa
Seronga
Selindu Spillway
ROUTE 18
Dobe
Nxaunxau
MABABE DEPRESSION
Etsha
MOREMI WILDLIFE RESERVE
Gumare
Okavango Delta
ROUTE 16
Nokaneng
AHA HILLS
Shorobe
ROUTE 15
DROTSKY'S CAVE
Maun
ROUTE 9
GCWIHABA HILLS
Tsao
Toteng
Makalamabedi
Sehithwa
ROUTE 14
Lake Ngami
ROUTE 10
MAKGADIKGADI GAME RESERVE
ROUTE 7B(2)
ROUTE 7B(1)
Rakops
Toromoja
Xhumo
Mopipi Dam
Groot Laagte
ROUTE 7A
D'kar
Deception
Deception Valley
ROUTE 3 & 12
Ghanzi
CENTRAL KALAHARI GAME RESERVE
Okwa
ROUTE 13
Takatshwaane Pan
Lone Tree
Metatswe
Ncojane
ROUTE 6 A
KHUTSE GAME RESERVE
ROUTE 1
Masetlheng Pan
ROUTE 6
Salajwe
Lehututu
Kang
Khudumelapye
Hukuntsi
Tshane
Lokgwabe
Mabutsane
ROUTE 4
Sekoma
Jwaneng
Khakhea
GEMSBOK NATIONAL PARK
Union's End
ROUTE 2
ROUTE 2, 6, 5
MABUASEHUBE GAME RESERVE
Werda
KALAHARI GEMSBOK NATIONAL PARK
Nossob Camp
Makopong
Bray
Nossob
Molopo
Auob
ROUTE 6
McCarthysrust
Bogogobo
Twee Rivieren Camp
Middlepits
Kolonkwaneng
Khuis
Rappel's Pan
Gakhibane
Vanzylsrust
Bokspits
Kuruman
ROUTE 5

Index

Hukuntsi 23
Lehututu 23
Lokgwabe 23
Mopipi 38
Otse 94
Shakawe 30
Tshane 23
Xhumaga 12, 13, 93
Visa requirements 80
Visitor requirements, customs 78–81

Waterholes 15, 16, 22

Water
  drinking 70
  driving through 91
Werda 12
Wild animals, feeding of 86
Woodland
  acacia 25
  western 25
Xai Xai 3, 4
Xakanaxa lagoon 54, 93, 145
Xumaga 12, 13, 93
Zonye Pan 36